FLIGHT OF THE STORK:
A Window of Experiences ~ In the Pursuit of Happiness
By Christopher Lane

Cover art by Christopher Lane   christopherboydlane@hotmail.com

Cover design by Todd Schafer   todd@schaferdesign.net

Edited by Kristin Kearns   kristin.kearns@gmail.com

ISBN: 978-0-615-24738-0

© 2008 by Christopher Lane. All rights reserved.

This book is dedicated to all people,

as we walk collectively toward our destiny.

CHAPTERS

1) Preface 1
2) The Incubator Baby 5
3) Faraway Father 7
4) Teen Oblivion 12
5) Punk Rock Family 15
6) Roots in the Ocean 19
7) The Conditioned Reflex 24
8) Cry of the Convicted 27
9) The Spiritual Awakening 32
10) New Beginnings 48
11) The Fashion Facade 51
12) Traveling: The School of Life 64
13) European Vacation 76
14) The Mysterious Woman
    Who Saved My Surf Trip 88
15) A Life Cut Short 97
16) The Guardian Angel Invoked 102
17) The Path of Yoga 108
18) The Kiss of Death in the Snow Park ... 111
19) Realizations in the Jungle 117
20) L'Eggo My Ego 128
21) Ethical Misconduct in the Realm of Saints ... 132
22) Reef Cuts and Bali Bombing 143
23) Zorba the Buddha 154
24) Dream Manifested 157
25) The Pancha Karma Experience 168
26) The Secret Revealed 181
27) Present Moment Awareness 185
28) The Pursuit of Happiness
    and Enlightenment 189

Preface

I'm offering this book not only as a reflection of my life, but also so that others may learn valuable lessons from my experiences. My life has been a grand adventure filled with the up-and-down cycles that we all go through on our personal journeys, and like everyone, I've made many mistakes that have caused me to suffer. Now I realize that through suffering and mistakes, we learn, and we can choose to grow from our mistakes or to relive them over and over, causing ourselves unnecessary misery.

I've come to believe that everything happens for a reason, and that we have the ability to design and sustain the landscape of our lives; our life is a garden that we plant, and with care and discipline, we can sustain it so that it flourishes in all directions. However, the environment that we're raised in has a direct influence on the way we evolve and the people we become. Growing up, I was ignorant to how my decisions affected me and everything around me, mainly because I didn't learn how to be an "ethical person" until the results of my actions forced me to do so. I turned

Preface

to spirituality for guidance and the growth of my inner garden. Each chapter I've written has a seed for change embedded in it, so that you too can cultivate your own spiritual garden.

Many ancient spiritual cultures and traditions have left us countless teachings regarding the pursuit of happiness and the reality and meaning of the universe's laws, which we cannot escape because we are interconnected with everything. Through the natural law of karma, we live the consequences of our thoughts, words, and actions. Ultimately, we create our reality through our choices, and happiness is a choice; we must have the intention, wisdom, and awareness to live it every moment of our lives.

I've written this book to show how these teachings and truths have come into my life and to share the tools, techniques, and methods I've learned and used to live a happier, more fulfilling existence. These include such proverbial principles as acceptance, compassion, forgiveness, gratitude, and unconditional love and kindness for all living beings, combined with the path and practice of yoga, meditation, and present moment awareness. On the path of self-discovery, I've learned that by utilizing these

Preface

gifts, I find meaning and purpose in my life, and I feel happier and more content on a moment-to-moment basis.

A timeless quote: "We're all doing the best we can for the level of awareness that we're at." This is a compassionate way to view ourselves and others, knowing that all of us want to be happy, loved, and accepted as we are. We often choose actions that lead us into suffering due to ignorance and ego. The ego is a product of the mind, and many spiritual traditions teach that it is the root of our dysfunctional perceptions of reality and the reason we feel separate from the Universe; for when we identify with the ego and the fluctuations of our mind, we lose touch with our true nature. I've never consciously wanted to suffer or cause myself pain or misery, although in many areas of my life, I have; but I've come to view past events as priceless teachings and opportunities for growth and change. In fact, many teachings regarding the path to happiness say that in order to find it, first we must suffer in the world of duality, for without one, how could we know the other?

Moving out of the past to become an authentically happy, enlightened person is my pursuit, and with this intention, I've found a door to a new relationship with life. Now, my

Preface

life path is to be of service to others in whatever way I can, which primarily involves being aware of how my thoughts, words, and actions affect me and those around me. Helping others is an innate human tendency, and the more we do it, the more contentment and joy we can experience. This can be something as simple as smiling at a stranger or helping someone in need, and it extends to dedicating ourselves to a cause for the benefit of humanity.

The world is changing dramatically, and a spiritual awakening is upon the human race. Writing this book has been a way for me to be a part of this movement, somehow and in some way, and also to review my past and to see how fortunate I am to still be here, able to share my life story with all who care to read it. Welcome to my shoes. I'm honored to be your host on the adventure of a lifetime.

~ Christopher Lane
  Santa Cruz, 2008

The Incubator Baby

My chaotic birth into this world was followed by nine days in an incubator; my parents could only touch me with thick plastic gloves, through openings in a lifeless glass box. I didn't have any way to bond with my mother, having been released from her safe womb and put on a life-support system devoid of human touch. I was a month premature and had a blood disorder, and I was in critical condition with the possibility of death. But for some reason, I was meant to live, and this was my first testament to that blessing, the divine gift of life.

I didn't learn until much later in my life, through deep meditation and introspection, that the reality of my first few weeks affected me in a myriad of ways: socially, emotionally, physically, and psychologically. My infantile fear of abandonment bled into a dysfunctional family life, and I turned to drugs and alcohol to numb my painful emotions. At a critical point, a guiding light shined on me and changed my perspective of who I was and the purpose of my life. This subtle awakening transformed my ignorance to awareness and set me on a path to self-discovery and growth. However, it would take many years to undo the pain that followed me from childhood into adulthood like a shadow.

It has been said that life is a precious gift and an opportunity to remember our divine spiritual nature. However, we're born into the world of object and form with amnesia to our past lives, who we are, and where we came from, and we are immediately conditioned by our family, culture, and society. Some spiritual traditions say that every soul chooses its own parents and birthplace, as we cycle through many lifetimes and are reborn based on our past-life karma. Maybe this was the life that my soul needed to experience in order to remember its true nature, and the suffering I've gone through will be a doorway to eternal peace and happiness.

Faraway Father

My first childhood memory is of my father leaning over my bed. His jet-black pompadour curled silently toward me like a wave as I looked on with a three-year-old's curiosity. A tear ran down his cheek and fell like a diamond onto my neck. It's one of the few times I can remember him crying.

"Your mother wants me to leave," he sobbed, staring at me as though I could understand his misery. Then he put his faded leather jacket on over his blue gas-station work shirt, and as he started to walk toward the front door, he looked back in remorse.

"Get out now, you lying bastard!" was my mother's response to his hesitation. The door slammed with a thunderous roar as he fled, not knowing where to go or what he'd do. He jumped into his 1964 cherry-red Mustang and sped off down the street.

What I remember most about my father was that he loved to watch television, work two jobs, smoke filtered Camel cigarettes, and fix up vintage cars and chopper motorcycles. He still had his Elvis pompadour from being a 1950s rebel without a cause, with scattered tattoos and sky-blue eyes.

He rarely showed emotion unless he was watching sports or a sitcom like *All in the Family* or tickling me sadistically. His long, greasy fingernails would dig into my sides as he tickled me until I started to half-laugh, half-cry, "Stop, Dad, stop!" He enjoyed this very much and would laugh to himself for a while longer after he stopped torturing me; afterward, he'd light up a cigarette and watch television in a tobacco trance.

I became addicted to nicotine at an early age as a result of his smoking in the car and leaving the windows rolled up; this resulted in childhood bronchitis and a love for the sweet, foggy aroma that surrounded our relationship. He used to take the family on long drives that were themselves as important as the destinations. Embedded in my mind is the memory of him taking out his upper set of false teeth and driving fast down the freeway, making strange sounds and comical faces to coax laughter out of my brother and me. He looked like a dried apple when he did this, and I laughed with the joy of a child being with his father.

He stopped collecting motorcycles after a gas tank exploded in flames beneath me on a drive around the neighborhood. He threw me off as we skidded to a stop, and as I hit cement I could see him running from the now flame-engulfed chopper. The next thing I remember is going to the hospital and being treated for minor scrapes and bruises. After the incident, Mom insisted that he sell all of his choppers. He reluctantly complied, and I never saw him ride a motorcycle again.

My parents had argued for as long as I can remember, and we moved from house to house, never calling a place home for long. Dad was always working, so I never knew when he was coming or going, but when he was home it seemed like my parents were always fighting about something. I became accustomed to this; at least Dad was home and we were all together. My brother would lock himself in his bedroom playing fantasy baseball and whispering, "Yes, another base hit!" to block out the screams and accusations.

One night when I was ten years old, Dad entered my bedroom as I was listening to my favorite Styx record. "I'm going on a long trip for work," he said emotionlessly. He came over to my bed, hugged me, and walked out of the room with a blank stare. "I hate you!" Mom screamed from the bedroom, sobs echoing behind her words. I knew he was going to his mail-order Filipino girlfriend's house, and that this time he wouldn't be returning. In a way, I was happy and thankful: Now I would be the one to sit in the comfortable reclining lounge chair in the living room and change the television channels. I had no conception of how the absence of a father figure in my life would shape me, or the harsh lessons I'd learn without a father's guidance.

During the time he was around, my father never had the ability to communicate with me about life or the difference between right and wrong, but he did teach me to play the typical American games of Ping-Pong, pool, and bowling. I also adopted his nervous leg movements and rare, unemotional smile. I remember, in fifth grade, the other kids laughing at me. "Look, he doesn't know how to smile," they mocked, making me self-conscious about my one-sided grin.

With my mom working full time and my brother wanting to be with his own friends without his little brother tagging along, I had to learn to raise myself after Dad left; and looking for attention and acceptance, I started hanging out with other disturbed youth. We'd drink hard liquor before our junior high classes, subconsciously trying to numb the pain of our dysfunctional families, and soon enough, I started getting into trouble in and outside of school. Frequent juvenile hall visits were the result of my reckless actions, and without the discipline and supervision of a father, I had no awareness of the consequences of the destructive path I was taking.

Teen Oblivion

We were in a poor financial situation after my parents divorced. Mom had to drive over the hill to work, a two-hour round trip on one of the most dangerous highways in California. After winding through the mountains at high speeds, part of the mass of humans racing each other to Bay Area offices, she'd come home stressed out and exhausted from the drive and job that she hated. But she did it to support my brother and me so that we could stay near the ocean and the friends that we had grown up with.

She'd often leave for the weekend to go on dates and have fun with her friends, needing some relief from her monotonous job and raising two boys alone. There'd usually be a twenty-dollar bill and a note on the counter reading: *Mom will be gone for a few days, here's $20 and there are Hungry Man dinners in the freezer. Love you!* This was fine by me; I'd watch MTV for hours, and my brother and I would have friends over, partying until late at night and getting up at the crack of dawn to go surfing in the icy Pacific Ocean.

Teen Oblivion

When my brother left for college, it was just Mom and I, and she insisted that I get a job if I wanted extra spending money. My first real job was at the fast food restaurant Jack-in-the-Box, where I had to wear tight blue jeans and a ridiculous-looking mesh hat. I worked forty hours a week doing a variety of jobs, from flipping burgers on the grill to dropping fries into liquefied lard. I also ate all of my meals there, an artery clogging perk, which started my long battle with teenage acne. I felt like a pimple-faced alien, and my self-esteem plummeted as other adolescents ridiculed my skin condition. My new job also funded my newfound marijuana addiction, and on the way home from work, I'd stop by my dealer's house next to the park and purchase a dime bag of weed. He was a Hells Angel type who reminded me of my dad, except instead of laughing at the television he'd laugh at me as I coughed my lungs out after taking hits from his skull bong. Since my dad had left the family, taking with him his cigarette-smoking habit, I began smoking marijuana to fill my life with another sweet aroma that reminded me of him.

I was getting high from the moment I awoke until right before bedtime, numbing the painful feelings and the confusion of my family life. Marijuana became the haze that filtered my reality, and a relatively harmless pacifier of the anger and sadness that I was feeling. Mom and I had arguments often, and these were what led me to hang out with my friends until late at night. I'd arrive home wasted, smelling like a skunk, and sneak up the stairs so as not to be questioned. Sometimes she'd catch and interrogate me in the worried tone of a mother, and if she happened to be drinking, the scene could have been straight out of the movie *Mommy Dearest*. I remember feeling, during this period of my life, like I was slowly drifting away from something deep inside me. I was on a downward spiral, unaware of the virtuous path that could lead to the love, joy, and contentment that were my true nature and birthright.

All in all, Mom did the best she could to raise two wild boys and still try to have a life of her own. She was a young, beautiful mother who was raised to get married at an early age and become a housewife. With her significant other gone and little financial help, she worked fifty hours a week, cooked delicious meals, and somehow managed to find time to take us on fun trips and vacations. Without a doubt, she was a superwoman, but I didn't realize this until later in life, when I let go of the anger and embraced the principles of forgiveness, acceptance, and gratitude.

Punk Rock Family

I was initiated into the world of hardcore punk rock at the tender age of thirteen. My brother and a friend had shaved their heads, a signature of the subculture, and when I insisted on mimicking my older sibling, they shaved off my long blond hair as we listened to Minor Threat. I liked the fast, rebellious, independent nature of the music, and I identified with the lyrics and felt energized when I listened to songs that questioned authority and the pursuit of the illusory American Dream. Through the music, I found a way to release my anger and grow as an individual, and I felt like I was part of an extended family of misfit youths.

My first attendance at a punk rock concert was in a run-down warehouse alongside the freeway: Circle Jerks, Scapegoats, and Free Beer were the bands that played in the dilapidated structure. The bouncer heckled my friend and me as we approached wearing bandannas and ripped clothing. "Where's your babysitter," he laughed sarcastically. He reluctantly let us inside after an older friend vouched for us, and as the powerful music started, I knew I had found a place that felt like home.

Punk Rock Family

With the typical 1980s "thrash" style of music, the mosh pit began: feral men and women with shaved heads and Mohawks, dressed in leather and boots, arms and legs flailing about. It was a dance of eccentricity and passive aggression, with humans going around in a circle to the fast grating guitar and deep drumbeat. I sat outside the circle, scared and hesitant to join in the counterclockwise whirlpool of bodies. But my rite of passage began as I was pushed into the pit from behind, dwarfed by the older, bigger punks, each doing their own unique movements. At first I just ran on the perimeter of the whirlpool of bodies, and then I began flapping my arms like wings, taking off to the music with a sense of freedom I had never felt before. Some people were diving off of the stage into the crowd. With arms held high, the jumpers would usually find a soft landing on a sea of hands, although some fell violently to the floor. At one point, as I was navigating the mosh pit's vortex, I fell down and waited to be trampled by the many black boots with silver spikes racing by my head. But in a gesture of comradeship, I was picked up and put on the shoulders of an unknown punk brother. Now many were climbing on the shoulders of others and doing a sort of dog fight in the air, still dancing around the circle, some laughing, others screaming the familiar lyrics of their favorite song.

As the bands changed, chaos erupted. People began crushing beer cans under their feet and throwing them at each other. Two sides were formed like a classic dodge ball game, except instead of rubber balls, there were razor-sharp aluminum cans flying at me from all directions. The sound of police sirens filled the air and the crowd dispersed. My friend and I ran as the riot police broke up the gathering before the headline band could play. We laughed about our wild night as we walked home, setting fire to some trash by the river for the hell of it. My initiation into the subculture was complete, and this was the beginning of a lifestyle that characterized my teenage years, giving me a foundation of individuality and self-expression amid the challenges of my young life.

But the alternative music scene wasn't accepted as it is today, and joining this movement made me an outsider to mainstream society. It was a rebellious act that allowed me to vent my storm of emotions, an outlet for the pent-up energy inside me. This lifestyle also inadvertently helped me to discover the creative side of my personality: A good friend and my brother and I created a local fanzine called *Disregarded*. It was a bimonthly publication dedicated to the punk rock music scene, and its pages were filled with pictures, interviews of prominent bands, record and gig reviews, comics and commentaries, and other topics related to the counterculture. Our high point was the opportunity to be interviewed by *Rolling Stone* magazine, but my brother thought that it would be "selling out," a cardinal sin of the faction, so it never came to pass. As time went on, we ran out of money to keep the periodical circulating, but publishing it was the beginning of my realization that I enjoyed writing and art as forums for self-expression.

Concurrent with this lifestyle, I had also started surfing, and as my love for the sport grew, I slowly transitioned from a punk rebel to a wave-chasing surfer. The lifestyles were complementary in some ways: The fast music fueled my passion for surfing, and both gave me a means for self-expression. And even though my outlook on life and my musical preferences remained the same throughout this transformation, a change of identity was set in motion as I was adopted by a new peer group.

Roots in the Ocean

As a young boy, I would look through surfer magazines, awed by the colorful pictures of men riding blue-green waves in distant lands. I could tell that it was a life of travel and adventure, freedom from the dreaded work-dedicated existence that my parents and all other adults seemed to be living. This way of life intrigued me, and I knew as I sat for hours, daydreaming of exotic destinations near and far, that this would be part of my destiny.

My brother bought an old, yellow surfboard at the flea market, and we tried it out at the surf spot where beginners go to learn the art and etiquette of wave riding. The cold Pacific Ocean and its fierce offshore winds froze my body instantly, and the waves were powerful and merciless. I could barely paddle the thick, banana-shaped surfboard, and whenever I tried to stand up on it, I fell over immediately into the icy water from lack of balance and coordination. I cursed the wretched sea and the men who sprayed me with water as I floundered in their way. I wore a black, beaver-tail wetsuit that I had bought used at a local surf shop, and it protected mainly my upper body, with a hanging tail that wrapped under the groin. My legs became frozen sticks within minutes of entering the ocean, and I looked like a penguin in my oversize jacket of rubber.

One day, as I was helplessly trying to dodge a breaking wave, I capsized in the lineup and swallowed a mouthful of water. My leash broke and my board smashed into the rocks while the older, experienced surfers heckled and threw rocks at me from the cliff. After my first few times surfing, what with the violent beatings from the waves and the surf culture's competitive, judgmental nature, I didn't think the sport was for me. However, the first time that I stood up on my surfboard and rode a wave for some distance, with the accompanying feeling of floating on a cloud, I knew that I was hooked for life. I had discovered another outlet for my energy, creativity, and anger, and as I remained passionate and disciplined, I fell in love with my newfound home in the sea.

The surfing scene of my generation encompassed all of the surfer lifestyles of the modern era, from longboarders to aerial acrobats to big wave enthusiasts. It was a time of heavy localism and cross-town rivalry among the surfing cliques. If you weren't from the area, or hadn't lived there for more than a few years, you had no chance of paddling out to any of the best spots and taking over the pack of local surfers. Most likely you'd be dunked underwater or, if you were lucky in the aggressive atmosphere, met with an escort to the beach.

Northern California surfers are a territorial bunch, and in the surf zone it's a fierce battle of every man for himself against the fifty-degree water, powerful waves, and hundreds of world-class surfers. Friends on land become competitors in the ocean, and only the dedicated and/or talented progress through the rivalry. It's often crowded in town, but for the adventurous, there is a multitude of outstanding breaks outside of the city limits, with not a soul in sight.

This is what my friends and I loved to do: travel up and down the coast to find secluded surf spots. We'd roll a thick joint of some stinky, green bud, roll up the windows, and smoke out the car as we listened to hardcore music to get our adrenaline going for the surf session. Sometimes our wetsuits would have been rotting in the trunk for a day or two, and we would grunt and whine as we pulled our cold, damp suits up over our mid-regions. But once our suits were on and zipped up, our misery transformed to warmth. We'd run down the beach hooting and hollering at the empty waves in the distance and take turns riding them after we paddled out through the turbulent whitewater, cheering one another on as we tried new maneuvers or suffered a horrible wipeout. Many of my fondest memories are of these carefree days of my youth, with just enough money to put gas in the car for local surfing excursions with my friends before or after school.

My family lived in Santa Cruz behind the West Coast's last beach boardwalk, and I traveled across town to attend high school on the eastside, wanting to go to the same school as my older brother. The seniors, jocks, and fashionable surfers called me a skinhead and harassed me any chance they got, but I had a group of friends of my own creed. In my freshman year, I was befriended by the loud-mouthed, white-haired brother of three talented surfers. He was a darling of the local surf crew because of his powerful presence, good looks, and comic nature. To befriend me, one day when I was sitting in the quad with my rebel brethren, he threw orange peels at my head. "Hey kook," he projected through the trees, from the area where the elite crew of surfers hung out. I let him pelt me with peels for about five minutes until my anger surfaced, and then I turned around to face him. He stood there with a big smile and introduced himself, extending his hand to me. We became inseparable friends, and my life changed drastically after I met him.

My white-haired friend loved to make up nicknames for people. Most surfers get one, usually an animal name of some sort based on the way they look or act. I was branded "the Stork" because of my long legs and towering height. I detested the name at first and would curse at anyone who called me by it, but this is how it usually happened: When your peers see your aversion to the name, they use it over and over again until it becomes part of your persona. "The Stork" eventually stuck to me like glue, whether I liked it or not. This was an initiation into the surfing community, and I would now associate myself with the values and code of ethics of this subculture. Thus began my new social identity, my fulfillment of the dream I'd had as a child to live the life of a surfer.

The Conditioned Reflex

On a typical weekend night out on the town, friends and I would attend parties and go crazy together drinking alcohol, snorting cocaine, smoking joints, and womanizing. We'd become animals as the night progressed, and this usually led to a fight or two to bolster reputations and egos. I was more of the quiet, shy type, but I enjoyed going out with my friends and being the one to roll the fattest joints in social settings.

One night in particular was a classic gathering, with all of the big-name surfers of that era, young and full of fire and intensity, joining to crash a university party. A pack formed to return to a party we had been kicked out of for being loud and obnoxious. As we pulled up to the house, twenty of us pouring out of a half-dozen cars, one of our crew picked up and threw a handful of rocks at the big bay window where all the college partygoers were standing, looking out at us. Before I knew it, the glass had shattered into a waterfall of small pieces, and a few brave students jumped out of the opening to defend their turf. A rumble ensued in the streets and front yard, fists flying in the darkness.

As I jumped out of the car, I saw one of my friends fighting someone and losing badly, so I ran over and helped him as any good, drunken friend would. The singer from the band that had been playing at the party saw the unfair two-on-one battle, and he came out of the shadows and punched me in the face, taking a chunk of skin off my forehead with his skeleton ring. Two others from my group jumped on him and kicked him to the ground as another challenger stepped up to fight me. We went head to head like boxers, and in my periphery I noticed that all of my friends were running down the street and jumping back into the cars. I then saw several police cars parked with their lights out, the cops inside watching the boxing matches and beat-downs. I ran with the fear of being left behind and yelled, "Wait!" as the last of my friend's cars started to pull away. I jumped through the back window, and my legs were still halfway out as we drove off. The boys were bloody, screaming, going into adrenaline fits reliving the experience, and laughing all the way home.

The Conditioned Reflex

This event epitomized my rebellious teenage years. I look back now and realize that I did these things to fit in and be accepted, and that the drugs and alcohol fueled my life-changing choices; I had no awareness of the disastrous consequences of my actions, which were driven by violence, anger, greed, and hatred. The Universe was guiding me in a compassionate way through these negative emotions even though, at that point in my life, I couldn't grasp that concept. My actions and choices would ignite karmic consequences that were ultimately a blessing in disguise, but first I had to suffer the fate of the seeds that I'd sown. I was now truly in the school of life, where brutal lessons were to be learned from ignorance.

Cry of the Convicted

My mom and her boyfriend, who had lived with us for three years, had had enough of my antics by the time I was eighteen, and they suggested that I find another place to live in the near future. I was hurt and confused; feeling rejected, I immediately moved into a small studio with a friend. I found a job at a local surf shop and worked five days a week to pay my bills and make ends meet. I all too soon realized how hard it was to live on my own, and how many things I'd taken for granted growing up under my parents' roof, things that were always available, like food, clean towels, and toilet paper. Our studio was the weekend spot for parties and get-togethers, and we'd drink all night and have sex with girls in rooms separated by hanging bedsheets. I was in my first long-term relationship at the time, but the social scene was just a recycled cesspool of people who had no respect for each other's feelings, which led to promiscuity and non-monogamy. It was a disgusting habitat after the clean, beautifully decorated house that I had lived in with my mom, but I was oblivious to my surroundings as I moved farther and farther into the world of drugs, alcohol, and random acts of stealing to support my habits.

The culmination of my thievery came when the owner of the surf shop where I was working fired me for stealing. Even though he couldn't prove anything, I was let go as an example to all the employees doing the same thing. In the weeks that followed, I went into a drinking binge, broke and jobless, drowning the emotional turbulence inside my mind. A few months went by, and without an income, I devised a plan of unwarranted revenge. I remember sitting on the cliff above the ocean and holding the gold key to the surf shop. Unknown voices screamed in my head to throw it, but bitter for having been fired, I decided to save it. This turned out to be the biggest mistake of my teenage years, and a karmic punishment for all of the wrongdoings I had committed. If only I had listened to the guiding voice of intuition that we all have but often dismiss, I would have saved myself from unimaginable suffering.

I moved back to my mom's house after running out of money and realizing that I couldn't go on living the way I had been. I knew that I needed help and counseling, and my mom knew it, too, so she agreed to let me move back home as long as I looked for another job and went back to school. Weeks later and for no apparent reason, I awoke in the middle of the night and decided to enact my plan of revenge: to break into the surf shop with the key I had saved. It had been months since I had been fired, and it was as if I was drawn by a force higher than myself. In a daze, I drove to the shop and parked behind it in the dark of the night. I unlocked the back door with the gold key, careful not to make any sound. Once inside, I grabbed a wetsuit and some clothes. The register was empty, so I left quickly after I heard a noise in the storage closet. I had a fearful premonition of getting caught, but now it was too late to escape my fate. I locked the door and sat behind the building in my car, uncertain whether to leave, crying for the deed I'd committed against a man who had given me a job and done nothing to justify this. In sudden terror, I noticed headlights from a vehicle screeching around the corner of the building.

    I started my car and sped away toward the ocean. The truck raced up behind me, and in my rearview mirror I saw that it was the owner of the shop; he smashed into my car and yelled profanities out of his window. There was a moment when I contemplated driving off the cliff to end my predicament, but instead I pulled over and waited for the beating that I knew I would receive. He opened my door and threw me onto the cement behind my car, and I lay there as he kicked and punched me, until the police pulled up and grabbed him off of me. "You little punk, how could you do this to me!" he screamed. I was handcuffed and taken downtown to the police station, where I confessed in tears of anguish and remorse.

Now I was a legal adult and had a criminal background for other minor offenses as a juvenile. The owner of the shop, a well-known figure in the surf community, went out of his way to tell everyone in town what I had done, and as a result, many people in the surf community rightfully disliked me. He did everything he could to prosecute me and make sure I received a stiff sentence, and mysteriously, my public defender changed multiple times throughout the trial. During the court proceedings, because I had confessed to the crime, the judge told me that he would let me out of jail early if I behaved myself, but that I was going to be sentenced to a year at the minimum-security correctional facility on the outskirts of town.

This would be a climactic turning point in my life; the bitter penalty for my actions led to a new awareness and a spiritual awakening. The reality of going to jail at nineteen years of age struck me like a sledgehammer, and the dreaded day came when I had to check myself into the correctional facility. I felt deeply lost in a river of fear and anxiety at the prospect of going to jail for so many months. Luckily, I was eligible for work furlough, where I'd be able to leave the compound on weekdays to work with a landscape company that had hired me a few months ago. The damage I had done to my life and reputation became all too real on the drive to the detention center; however, the tide was turning in the sea of fate, and although I couldn't see it, there was a silver lining to this cloud of consequences.

The Spiritual Awakening

My mom dropped me off at the barbed-wire-fenced entrance to the local minimum-security jail for nonviolent offenders. As I walked into the yard where prisoners of every race and color comingled, I realized that I was most likely one of the youngest there, and this wasn't going to be easy time. But I was a survivor, and I would survive among men who were locked up for heinous crimes unknown to me; I was naive to the life that would confront me behind these walls.

"You're a full-fledged convict now," the jail warden scoffed. I was given my bunk assignment and escorted to the locker at the foot of my new bed. It was an upper bunk with a thin, lifeless mattress shabbily covered by a stained blanket. The pillow was small and smelled like a mixture of mold and the countless faces that had lain on it. "If a jail-issued pillow could talk, I wonder what stories it would tell," I pondered as I cried myself to sleep on my first night in the personal hell I had created.

The days that followed were shocking and miserable as I tried to cope with where I was. I didn't want to take a communal shower because I had heard all of the stories about the sexual abuse in that unguarded area, so I waited until nobody was taking one. During an evening break I saw my opportunity. There wasn't a soul in sight, but it looked like someone had left one of the showers running behind a shoulder-high wall at the far end. I hastily disrobed and headed toward the running shower; there was steam coming off of it, so I figured I could jump in and out without any downtime waiting for the water to get hot. As I rounded the corner, I was confronted with the most horrific sight I had ever seen.

I looked down to see a man with only one arm and no legs. His prosthetic legs were propped up against the wall as he washed himself, and he grunted in disapproval at my intrusion. "Sorry, I didn't see you," I said with my head down, realizing that wasn't the best thing to say. He slithered away on his stubs to put on his makeshift legs, and I turned on another shower and doused myself with cold water, which felt refreshing after such a shocking experience.

The Spiritual Awakening

Then lunchtime arrived, and hundreds of inmates stood scowling, posturing, and stink-eyeing one another while waiting in line for their meal. I waited in my jail-issued tan pants and matching shirt, but I stuck out like a sore thumb with my long, sun-bleached hair and surfer-boy features. "I can't believe they let little maggots like you in here," mocked a snaggle-toothed man standing behind me. Many laughed, and I turned away humiliated. The jeers continued as we shuffled toward the food, which was served by inmates with large steel spoons and metal tongs. I received my portion of what looked like barf on a plate and looked for an empty seat at one of the crowded tables. I found a corner open and politely asked if I could sit down.

"Yeah, sure," one man mumbled, and the other dozen men briefly looked at me as I sat down and started to eat.

"What you in here for, boy," asked a man sitting across from me.

"Petty theft," I offered, not wanting to go into detail. "I've got a year, but they say I'll get out in three to four months if I do good time."

He smiled and returned to greedily slurping his food, but I felt relieved by even such a small sign of acceptance by these individuals.

The Spiritual Awakening

The first weekend, my girlfriend was able to visit me. Most inmates had someone visiting them, and many looked and whistled as she walked toward the visiting area, where I was seated on the grass. We were allowed to hug and kiss briefly, but no fondling or making out was permitted. I saw the guard walk around a corner out of sight, so I put my hand up her top to feel the perky breasts that I had been dreaming about. I felt the sting of a whip on my shoulder. Another guard had been hiding behind a tree and seen my inappropriate behavior; he picked me up by the neck and yelled in my face, "That's it! She's not allowed to visit you for a month." They led me away without allowing me to say goodbye to her, and she waved as I disappeared into the shadows of the inner compound walls.

After the second week, I went on work furlough, and I was given a small sack lunch for the day. When I picked it up from the kitchen basket, I looked inside to see a junior-sized sandwich, a small bag of chips, and an apple the size of a walnut. I had a big appetite and knew that wouldn't be enough food for me to make it through the ten-hour workday. No one was around, so I picked up an extra banana, put it in my bag, and started to sneak away.

The Spiritual Awakening

"Hey you, come here!" an unseen guard shouted from the central corridor. "Give me your lunch bag right now!" he ordered as I stood in front of the half-open window to his office. He looked inside the bag and grabbed the extra banana, and before I could react, he wound up like a pitcher in the big leagues and threw it at me. It felt like a real baseball as it hit me square in the face. Soft banana exploded all over me as I fell to the ground, seeing stars. "You ever do that again and you're going to lose your work furlough, you little thief," he spat, his face boiling red and eyes filled with anger.

"I thought that they were there to take. It's my first work furlough day," I pleaded from the ground. The other inmates in the breakfast line were in fits of laughter after witnessing the banana-bashing incident. I regained my composure, wiped off the yellow slime with my shirt, and walked over to the ten-speed bicycle I had brought to ride to work.

I worked all day in the hot sun, landscaping and planting a wildlife restoration project on an abandoned landfill site. I'd get so famished during the day, working hard and sweating in the sun, that by the time I returned to jail in the evening I'd be half starved and ready to eat whatever they'd serve me in the kitchen. Work furlough guys got a special meal and ate together in the evenings, separate from the other inmates. The food was well prepared and usually tasted decent.

One evening I returned from work to a special dinner of pizza. The cheesy slices were delicious, and after I devoured my portion I greedily returned for seconds. "Sorry man, there's only one piece left and we're saving it for the guy who hasn't returned from work," the food server stated in a monotone. It was almost closing time, so I said, "OK, but if you're going to close down and that's a leftover, I'd be happy to eat it." Within a few minutes, the server whistled at me to take the last piece, which I happily devoured. As I stuffed the final bite of crust into my mouth, I saw the last work furlough man pull up on his bicycle. As he rushed in for his serving, I got a bad feeling in my stomach.

"What, that little shit ate my piece of pizza!" he squealed in my direction. The fight-or-flight syndrome activated in my nervous system, and I started to regurgitate the pizza as the pissed-off man came storming over. "I'll get you back, you greedy little pig," he hissed, while a few men around me said, "Uh-oh" and "Serves you right."

The Spiritual Awakening

As the days passed, I would see the vengeful man in different parts of the detention center and outside, where people played sports or lounged in the sun. He would stare at me from afar, and I could see him talking to his friends and pointing in my direction. I tried to stay very aware of what this guy was plotting, but I knew that it would be some type of surprise attack.

A few weeks later, they were serving deep-fried fish sticks for our work furlough dinner and giving everyone two servings. I knew one of the guys serving the fish sticks, so I felt safe eating what he gave me, and he picked out a couple of big pieces and put them on my metal serving plate with a smile. I gobbled them quickly as usual and noticed that the food workers behind the kitchen counter were laughing and having a great time joking with each other. It lightened my mood, too, and after I ate I took off to shower and go to bed.

I found just a few men showering. I had learned to take my clothes off and jump under a shower without looking scared or self-conscious. I was ready to defend myself against any unwanted advances, but most of the men were not sexual predators, just there to do their time. My stomach felt full, and I burped the taste of fish sticks as I stood under the hot water. I dried off and started to feel faint on the way to my bunk, and when I lay down, I was feverish and had a splitting headache. Within minutes I knew that I was going to throw up, so I rolled out of my bunk and ran to the toilet. Fish sticks and stomach fluids exploded in a projectile of vomit into the stinky bowl of the toilet. After I stopped vomiting, I had the sudden realization that I was going to explode from another orifice, and I nearly lost consciousness from the draining experience. Finally, I made it back to my bunk, drenched in sweat and shivering in pain. I passed out but woke many times during the night to relive the initial occurrence, and I had to call in sick to work the next day because I could barely get out of bed. Other men in the detention center had had the flu recently, so I surmised that I had also acquired it, and although it passed in a few days, I was weak and feeble for weeks to come.

Weeks passed by slowly, but thankfully I was working three to five days a week and saving some money for after my release. For the first time in my life, I was starting to appreciate the things that I had always taken for granted:

mainly my freedom, but also family, friends, and the laid-back surfing lifestyle. All these things had been stripped from me during my incarceration, which was the consequence of my many misguided choices. It was also the result of growing up in a dysfunctional environment without a father and hanging out with other disturbed individuals; mixing that with drugs and alcohol had led to careless decisions and ignorant behavior. I was becoming aware of the natural law of karma through trial and error, and I had a lot of time to reflect on the actions that had put me in jail.

My mom had dropped off a book for me: *The Way of the Peaceful Warrior* by Dan Millman. I read it in twenty-four hours, absorbing every word, touched by the story that would profoundly change my life forever. Reading the book gave me a new understanding of life, a spiritual and inspiring perspective on how to live the life of a peaceful warrior. My interpretation of a peaceful warrior was someone who viewed life as a spiritual academy and created a peaceful existence for himself and others through ethical choices and actions. This was my first glimpse into being aware of my every thought, word, and action, and that there was a consequence for everything I did in my life (karma). A door had opened to a new world, even though I was still living the karmic consequences of my past mistakes. I felt that I had suffered deeply on many levels at a young age, and the reading and rereading of this book while I was in jail was the beginning of a new paradigm. Now I had a blueprint for a way to live that would alter the self-destructive course I was on, and I vowed to become a better person and live the teachings of the transformative book.

After three months I was eligible to be released on good time, and I was waiting for the day when the guard would shout over the loudspeaker, "Roll it up!" They yelled this when a person was to roll up his bedding and depart. Whoever was being released got the biggest smile on his face, oozing with excitement to be finally free from the dark, musty corridors. Every man must have felt envy when shaking the hand of a soul departing from the purgatory we had created for ourselves, where we wished and waited for our time to be served.

I had been through a lot in the three months that I'd been incarcerated, and I was dedicated to finishing my time simply working, reading, and relaxing on my bunk until they called for me to return to the outside world. I had received a prose poem entitled "Desiderata," about attaining happiness in life, and I was reading another great book about the life of Gautam Buddha. The Buddha's journey to enlightenment, which has affected and transformed millions of people, awoke something deep inside me, and I was intrigued by his teachings of the Eightfold Path and the Four Noble Truths. He left these teachings to guide each and every person out of suffering and enable us to realize our true nature. Becoming enlightened, as I understood it then, meant that you would transcend the world of duality into nirvana, but that you could also choose to return to the earth plane to help others achieve self-realization. It was the perfect book to read in my current environment, even though it was difficult for me to grasp all of the spiritual concepts at that point in my life.

One day when I was deep into the book, a man who had just returned from work furlough came over to my bunk and asked me what I was reading. I wasn't in the mood to talk or be distracted, but I briefly explained what I was reading and then went back to the enlightening story. Out of my periphery, I saw him stick his cigarette package under my mattress and pull out his last cigarette. He then walked away quickly as a guard came strolling up to my bunk. "Looks like a drug transaction," the guard hissed at me with contempt.

"I'm reading my book. That guy just said hello and walked away," I retorted.

The guard reached for the cigarette package under my bunk and opened it, revealing a half-smoked joint hidden in the bottom. A dark fear overcame me; I knew that if anyone was caught with drugs, their good time would be revoked, and they would be sent downtown to the county jail, which was considered "hard time" compared to the minimum-security jail. The guard looked at me with a grin of evil delight, ordered me off of my bunk, and cuffed my hands behind my back. "You're going to the blue room and will be processed downtown," he stated after reading me my rights. I begged him to believe that I'd had no idea that there had been a joint inside the cigarette package. But he wasn't listening or sympathizing. He walked me through the compound to be deposited in the well-known blue room.

The metal door slammed. I'd be kept in the holding cell before being shipped downtown. I had heard stories of the blue room and its one tiny window, out of which you could see the police van coming to take you to a new level of hell. On the walls there were graffiti of figures deranged and horrific, and writings of despair and anger from the many who had found this room their temporary fate. I sobbed in agony at the prospect of losing my good time and having to spend another nine months downtown. I was so overwhelmed with emotions that I became suicidal. I took off my watch and tried to slit my wrists with the steel part of the band. I was barely able to puncture my skin with the dull edge, and I fell to the floor weeping in misery. I would definitely lose my girlfriend if I had to spend nine more months in jail. She seemed more distant as the months passed, rarely answering her phone or returning my calls.

And then I had a sudden intuition that everything would be OK, that there were better times ahead. This was my compassionate inner guide, speaking to me on a level that was more of a feeling than words heard in my mind. I stood up from the cold, cement floor and peered out of the small window at the parking lot where the police wagon would pick me up. The lot was empty, so I sat back down and tried to calm my mind, take deep breaths, and remember the teachings and practices of *The Way of the Peaceful*

The Spiritual Awakening

Warrior and the life of the Buddha. As I sat in the blue room, praying for and visualizing my freedom, minutes seemed like hours. Finally, the guard opened the door and led me out of the holding cell. Unpredictably, he walked me back over to the main building, un-cuffed me, and told me to go back to my bunk. I was told that I would be taking a urine test to see if I had drugs in my system, and that was it! I was ecstatic and immediately thought, "Did the positive thinking, praying, and visualizing of my freedom help my situation?" Of this I wasn't sure, but I was overjoyed that I wouldn't lose my good time and be sent downtown for a crime I didn't commit.

The drug test was given the next day, and I was scared as I urinated into the plastic bottle. I had been smoking pot consistently for years and wasn't sure how long it stayed in your system, but I had no choice. I filled the bottle to the top; I had been drinking extra water to dilute any residue of the past. My work furlough had been suspended until the test results came in, and now I had to move to the other side of the wall to bunk with those unable or not approved to have a job outside of the compound. I became even more silent and reclusive, reading my book and going outside only for a little exercise besides meals and bathroom breaks. To make matters worse, my friend who worked in the kitchen told me that he had been forced to give me fish sticks that had been soaked in urine and poisonous substances by the guy whose pizza I had eaten. I had known that the surprise attack would take place, and in a way I was relieved, hopeful that the payback I'd received was the worst of it.

A few days later, I was sitting outside in the sun, dreaming of perfect waves and friends rejoicing as they ran down the beach to paddle into the green-hued ocean, when two guards walked over to the man who had slid the roach under my bunk. They handcuffed him and read him his rights before walking him out of sight, and I got a knot in my stomach as I heard my name called over the podium loudspeaker. I walked the walk of one unaware of his fate. With my head down, I stood in front of the guard's podium window. "Your good time is being reinstated, and you're going to be released as planned this weekend," the guard said, and I detected my first sign of friendliness. I felt like an energy ball was going to explode inside me as I walked away, and I silently praised whatever higher source had saved me from rotting for another nine months in jail.

The Spiritual Awakening

Finally, the day came when my name was announced over the loudspeaker and I was told to "roll it up," as I had heard so many times before. I wondered how the men felt who had been in there for years and were looking at more to come. I shook hands with the friends I had made. Regaining my freedom was the happiest moment of my life. I knew that I had been given another chance to change, and I was committed to a new direction and to becoming a better person.

I had learned extremely valuable lessons in jail, and I'd had my first awakening and guidance toward being a conscious individual. The books I had read on spirituality and self-growth had been the counsel that I had never found in family or friends. I now understood karma: how every thought, word, and action has a consequence and how I had created all of the suffering I was experiencing. I was like a newborn child, unable to see and comprehend my new reality, but my eyes were opening and a new path had begun.

New Beginnings

Now, with my personal freedom reinstated, I decided to take some classes at the junior college to explore my passion for art and writing. I made a solid commitment to myself to never again steal anything from anyone, for any reason. I also vowed to stop hanging out with the guys that I had been getting into trouble with. I knew that in order to change my habits, I needed to surround myself with well-respected, positive people who loved, supported, and accepted me for who I was and the mistakes I'd made.

I worked odd jobs and stayed focused in school, and went surfing with friends on a daily basis. The friends who really knew me, and who knew that I was making a big effort to change my life, took me under their wings of compassion and understanding and guided me toward an ethical life. My white-haired friend and I spent most of our time laughing in a perpetual surf-a-thon that entailed surfing twice a day and living a relatively happy and carefree existence. An influential person in the surfing community, he backed me up in any and all dramatic social situations that I encountered because of my past. He believed in me and knew that I had made mistakes like everyone else, but I had paid for my errors and was ready to move on. Still, in small communities, the inhabitants usually remember the mistakes made by each individual, and people generally know of each other from gossip. And no matter how much I tried to live an honest and moral life, my negative reputation would follow me for years to come.

As time passed and I surrounded myself with positive, good-natured friends living principled lives, the ghosts of the past were exorcised. With this new family of friends, I started to gain more self-confidence and clarity on my path, even though many more trials and tribulations were to come. Throughout all of the drama I created for myself, I was a die-hard surfer, one of the breed that chooses surfing for life—not to compete in contests or to have pictures taken of me, but because of the connection I had with the ocean and the feeling I got from riding waves. It's a personal bond that a surfer has with the ocean, and for me it was a place of refuge, a home away from home. I was grateful to be given another chance in the community, even though I was still paying a karmic debt for the things I'd done.

New Beginnings

My studies and spiritual realizations from the books I'd read in jail kept me focused on what it was to be a good person. Teachings of ethical and moral conduct were at the forefront of my understanding, which involved being aware of every thought, word, and action and how they affect me and others. I'd learned other teachings and concepts that would later have a positive influence on my life, but they would have to be lived and learned many times before I could be aware of their true meaning and apply the principles to all aspects of my life. Many more challenging situations were to come, and these would shape my destiny and further set me on a course to self-discovery and the realization of my true nature.

The Fashion Facade

In my early twenties, my love of movies and theatre led me to an interest in acting, and an opportunity arose for me to step into a transparent world of bright lights and superficial icons. I was looking for a way to express my creativity and pain, and I saw acting as the ultimate human expression whereby you could play many roles and not be restricted to one character. I was still searching outside of myself for acceptance, love, and understanding; I didn't yet realize that in order to receive these things from others, first you must give them to yourself.

I called an acting school to inquire about their program, and I made an appointment for a consultation to discuss the details. I met with the director of the school, who liked my look and asked me if I also had any interest in modeling. I didn't think that I was model material, but being tall and having an interest in acting, I spontaneously said, "Yeah, sure." I ended up taking their three-month program for acting and modeling, where I discovered a talent for both. The program showed me the ins and outs of the industry, and dynamic classes taught by professionals in the field offered me the experience and confidence to pursue this line of work.

After I graduated from the program, I was advised to try to get representation from the best agency in San Francisco, so I drove up for an open call. If they were willing to see me, this would be where I'd show my amateur photographs. That day it was raining hard, and my beat-up Dodge Dart barely made it through the torrential downpour. But I felt that something extraordinary was calling me, and I laughed with resolve as I hydroplaned down the freeway toward my fate.

Once I'd arrived at the agency, I gave my amateur snapshots to the secretary and waited in the crowded lobby. One by one, the others waiting for the open call were turned down with a "Thank you for coming," delivered by the cute but pretentious secretary. I sat in an uncomfortable wooden chair, extremely anxious, the last one waiting to be accepted or rejected by the fashion demigods. The secretary approached me with a smile and said that the agents wanted to see me. I was surprised. My heart started beating quickly, but I remembered a Buddhist teaching on how our bodies and emotions can be regulated by focusing on the breath, so I slowly inhaled and exhaled to center myself. I walked into the agents' office, where they all sat around a glass table and did their bookings. I was introduced to the agency's founder and asked to have a seat. The founder was a short man with a feminine voice. He wore designer glasses and had a cat-sized dog on his lap.

"You have a great look," he said with delighted fervor and a quick smile. "How would you like to be a BIG star?" He merrily enunciated BIG.

"That would be great," I nervously replied, not knowing what to say or how to react in front of this legendary agent.

"Well, my boy, our contract is a handshake and a smile," he announced as he put his multi- ringed hand out to me. "And here's a list of photographers to do test shoots with; we'll be calling you shortly," he added as he walked me out of the office. "This is Fluffy," he said, as his petite dog jumped out of his arms to the ground. "Do you really want to be a BIG star?" he asked again, with the eyes of a man who had started countless careers in the fashion world.

"Uh, well yeah," I replied cautiously, standing awkwardly and starting to sweat in my thick wool sweater.

"Then take Fluffy for a walk around the block to do her duty," he ordered, knowing that I wouldn't refuse if I wanted to start our relationship off on a good note.

The Fashion Facade

I was still in shock from being accepted by one of the biggest agencies in San Francisco, and now I had to walk a little dog with a studded pink collar around busy Union Square. As I exited the wobbly elevator onto the street, which teemed with traffic and hordes of people, Fluffy started viciously barking, and everyone looked and laughed at me and the dog with the bad attitude. I walked as fast as I could with my head down in embarrassment and let Fluffy do her duty at the base of a tree. I then returned to the eighth-floor office, and Fluffy barked in gratitude as I handed her leash to the secretary. I gathered my information packet and list of photographers and left with a big smile, elated with my accomplishment.

That day heralded a life-changing event. Soon I would enter the world of modeling and acting and discover the shady reality of those industries. It took a while for the fact to sink in that I was being represented by an agency whose models and actors were held in the highest esteem, an advantage in this competitive field of work. Within a few days, I had called multiple photographers to set up appointments to start building my portfolio, and I felt that this career path could set me in a positive direction.

The Fashion Facade

After my test shoots, I ordered my first composite card highlighting my best pictures, and it was sent out to all of the agencies' clients and industry contacts. I immediately received a flattering response and started getting bookings for print and runway jobs, as well as landing two national commercials, which meant I was now a member of the Screen Actors Guild. I started making good money and was staying out of trouble, and the work was easy and came naturally to me. Driving my old Dodge Dart to San Francisco took an uncomfortable hour and a half on fast-paced highways, and after driving back and forth for a few months, I decided to move up to the City to be more readily available for the daily calls from my agency.

The booking agent in charge of my agency's men's division had a room available; it was a great situation, since she was well connected in the fashion business and liked me enough to let me move into her house. After I moved into the windowless back room, I started getting booked consistently, mainly doing fashion shows because of my height, and I planned to go to Europe to try my luck in the big leagues of the fashion world. The dark side of my success was that I became narcissistic from constantly being looked at and critiqued by people in the business.

The Fashion Facade

Even though I was working a lot, for every job I acquired, I was turned down for many others, and the hollow attitude of the clients and agents during the go-sees and castings made me feel like a piece of meat in a display counter.

Despite the shallowness of the process, things were looking bright for me. I felt like I had pulled myself out of the gutter and changed my life in a beneficial way. I was living in a multicultural, eclectic city, where my mom's side of the family had lived for four generations, and I was able to support myself financially. Spiritually, I was growing and learning more every day from the transformative books I'd continued to read. I was also becoming more aware of the fact that when you embark on a path of morality, you will be tested until you understand the meaning of the lessons you've learned. This added a sense of adventure to my new life, and I felt that I was ready for whatever future challenges I'd face.

My next wave of emotional turbulence started at the height of my career, when I was contacted by a self-proclaimed "Manager of the Stars" from New York City. He called me one day as I was lounging at home after a surf session. I had just taken a bong hit. "May I speak to Christopher?" he asked in a calculated voice.

"This is him," I replied, and coughed to clear the residual smoke from my lungs.

"I received your modeling card and am very impressed with your work. I'm a manager affiliated with the biggest agencies in New York City, and I wanted to talk with you about your budding career," he stated professionally.

"Wow, well, I have an exclusive contract for fashion and commercial bookings with my agency. You should probably contact them," I managed to articulate despite my stoned stupor.

"I just want to tell you that I think you're the next Tom Cruise and that I can get you a role in a major motion picture," he proclaimed in an important tone. I decided to end the conversation politely, as I was too stoned to believe what he was saying.

"By the way, how did you get my home phone number?" I asked before I hung up.

He replied that he was in contact with my friend from acting school who, after graduation, had gone to the open call at my current agency and been refused representation. He came from a wealthy family and had an inflated ego, and he was bitter that I, unlike him, had been accepted. I

The Fashion Facade

thought it strange that he would give out my phone number to a manager knowing that I already had representation, so I decided to call him to see what was going on with this strange character from the East Coast.

I called him the next day, and he eagerly informed me that this manager from New York City was affiliated with all the premier agencies, directors, and bigwigs in the fashion industry. "I talked to him too, and he said that he loves your look and wants to fly both of us out to New York to meet some of his clients!" The story was becoming a bit bizarre, but being naive to the derangement in the fashion world, I was hoping that this manager wasn't a fraud, and that he might be able to help me take my career to another level as he had promised.

The manager began calling me every night. He told me to call BMW dealerships because he was going to buy me a car, and also that he was looking for a home to buy in San Francisco, and I could live there for free. He sounded authentic and convinced me with names of actors and celebrities that he managed, and I became completely awestruck, believing everything this unknown person was telling me. I called my agent and told him that I wanted to have this man as my manager, even though I had an exclusive contract with my home agency. My agent was upset and said that they didn't like managers, and that if I was going to go that route, then our agreement and relationship would be terminated. I thought about it for a while, and after I made the decision to be represented by the New York City manager, my agency let me go. This wasn't what I'd wanted to happen, but I had high hopes that my new manager would make my acting and modeling careers take off. I was star-struck and felt that I had made a wise decision, even though I was now on my own, without the guiding hand of the agency that had started my career.

A few weeks later, after not hearing from my new manager in a week or so, I received a call from the guy who had introduced him to me. "Oh man, I heard that our manager in New York City is really a porno king who has his own film company, and that he works with the big agencies and lures the models that are struggling to get work to do his XXX- rated movies!" he exclaimed. I tried to comprehend what he was saying. "I guess he just got busted for something and is in a lot of trouble," he announced vindictively, knowing that I had been dropped from the agency that had rejected him. The realization hit

The Fashion Facade

me that I had been utterly lied to and misled, and now I was in a dire situation, broke and without an agency to get me work. The stardom, the car, the house—everything the manager had promised me had just been a smokescreen to lure me, most likely, into his pornographic films, but fortunately it hadn't gone that far.

In desperation, I concocted a plan of revenge that I hoped would pay for the damage he had done to my livelihood. The next day, I decided to write the porno king a letter and tell him that I was going to sue him if he didn't compensate me monetarily for the irreparable harm he had done to my career by deceiving me. I made the unwise choice of untruthfully writing that my former agency was backing me in the lawsuit against him. By doing this, I was now going against the spiritual laws and teachings that I had been studying: that revenge and dishonesty always result in more suffering. This mistake would ignite the fire of disaster that would cost me all I had worked for and more.

My roommate, who still worked for my ex-agency, came home crying one day. She started yelling that they had received a call from one of their affiliate agencies in New York City about my inflammatory letter to the porno king.

The Fashion Facade

This man was apparently connected to them and some of their clients, and they were taking the situation very seriously. I had written the letter out of desperation and really hadn't thought that I'd get a response, let alone a drama like this! My roommate informed me that I would have to move out immediately. She also demanded that I write a legal letter stating that I had lied about my ex-agency backing me in the lawsuit and that I wasn't going to pursue any legal action. She stated emphatically that I was now blackballed from working in San Francisco, which meant that no agency would take me in, and I wouldn't be able to get any work in the city. I was devastated. My dreams were shattered. I had been taken advantage of due to no wrongdoing on my part except gullibility; nevertheless, I had compounded the situation with vengefulness and lies. It was an abrupt ending to my newfound career, but I tried to stay optimistic that something good would come from this episode.

After writing my letters of apology to all concerned, and before I moved out, I decided to shop around the city for another agency. But every agent knew who I was, as word travels quickly in the fashion world, and they all dismissed me with a smug response: "We'll get back to you." I did end up finding a small agency that liked my book and decided to give me a chance, and for this I was grateful, although in order to save money, I had to move back to Santa Cruz and commute to the city again. As an experienced model in a small agency, I was booked for most of their jobs, but the work was scarce and I had to start thinking about going back to school or getting a part-time job to support myself.

Within a few months, not sure of my direction, I decided to take an aptitude test after a friend told me about the great opportunities the Coast Guard offered. My test score was in the high 90s out of 100, and the Coast Guard recruiters called me relentlessly, trying to get me to commit to a four-year term and officer training. I pondered this huge life decision and ran it by a few good friends that I regarded as intelligent and worldly. Their suggestion was that I forget about the Coast Guard, sell everything I had, and go on an extended surf trip out of the country. This did sound a lot better than going to boot camp and being ordered around like a child. So I abandoned that plan and started the process of selling my car and my belongings at the flea market to finance a surf trip to a yet-unknown international surf destination.

The Fashion Facade

My friends had invaluable experience traveling the globe on surfing adventures, and they informed me of the many benefits of traveling, for the first time leaving the nest that is home to go out into the world. In fact, it was the greatest gift that I'd ever received: being encouraged to go on an international journey alone so that I would learn priceless lessons as I transformed into an adult.

I was reading an assortment of spiritual and self-help books and embracing the mindset that everything happens for a reason, trying to see the bright side of every event. These concepts gave me a feeling of peace when I applied them to challenging everyday situations, and slowly but surely my attitude was changing, allowing me to view my life as a great blessing that was unfolding perfectly, whether I knew it or not. Applying these principles eased the disappointment I felt after the destruction of my acting and modeling career. Leaving it all behind, I'd embark on a life-altering journey that would ignite my flame for traveling the world and teach me valuable lessons in the process.

Traveling: The School of Life

As I considered my options for where to travel outside of the environment I'd grown up in, I heard a few interesting stories from friends who had been going to wave-rich, tropical Central American countries. This was when a variety of wars and rebellions were taking place in Latin America, and it wasn't the popular tourist destination that it is today. The thought of going there on a surf trip was intriguing, a magnificent adventure for my first international journey. I had sold everything I owned to finance the trip—my car, old clothing, and other assorted goods—and I left a little savings in the bank so as to have something to return to, or in case of an emergency on the road. I prepared by reading a book on Central America's customs, and I bought my plane ticket to my imagined paradise. Planning the journey was an exhilarating experience, and at the airport my mind raced with visions of what was to come. As the plane took off, I felt like a child again, in search of new horizons and unfamiliar experiences. My heart beat with excitement as we soared through the sky, and I dreamt of the endless possibilities of what could happen on my first global excursion away from home.

I didn't speak any Spanish except "buenos días" and "gracias," the typical first words learned by North Americans, also affectionately known as "gringos." But I had a book on the Spanish language, and I was studying it so that I would be able to converse with the locals. I was told by my worldly friends that locals would be more willing to take me in and introduce me to their culture and traditions if I was alone and willing to learn their language.

As we landed in the dilapidated Central American airport, I reminded myself to stay open to the many beneficial opportunities that may arise in this new country, but to also look at people and situations with the third eye of caution and intuition. As I disembarked the air-conditioned airplane into the balmy climate, it was as if I had entered another world. Confusion and excitement mounted as I took the first steps of my adventure, and I knew that this was a turning point in my life.

I had made plans to go to a small Caribbean town where a friend of mine had a hotel, and a few other friends were reported to be staying there and surfing the legendary Hawaii-like waves. The surf was said to break over a sharp coral reef and have perfect, hollow waves that connected for three long sections, which meant the possibility of a long ride. It was still a relatively unknown area to surf, and I had no idea what to expect.

I grabbed my surfboards and overstuffed backpack, which came out on a shredded circular conveyor belt, and went through immigration without a problem. The immigration officer simply smiled at me, showing all of his teeth, and said, "Bienvenidos!" As I walked out of the main corridor of the airport and onto the street, I was smothered by a dozen taxi drivers and other vendors offering their services. "Where are you going, amigo," and "You need a taxi, my friend," they shouted in broken English, trying to out-hustle each other to be the object of my attention. I managed to work my way over to an isolated area underneath a majestic palm tree, to regroup and take time to choose which of these individuals would give me insight and guide me on the first steps of my journey.

A young Latino approached me and asked in good English where I was going. I felt a good vibe from him, and he offered to travel with me on the eight-hour bus ride to the town where I was going, to make sure that I made it to my destination safely. The bus fare was cheap, so it seemed like a good plan, and we departed for the small Caribbean fishing village on a rickety bus packed with locals and their many possessions. I was smashed in the back of the bus, along with a rather large, sweaty woman and her four children screaming and making faces at me. They teased me in words that I didn't understand, so I just looked out the window into the thick jungle canopy as we sped through the mountains. The driver was dangerously passing other buses and narrowly dodging gigantic potholes and iguanas on the partially paved road. Luckily, my new friend was in the seat in front of me, and he gave me some invaluable information about his country and what to do and not to do—important rules of the road such as "Never let your backpack out of your sight" and "Put all of your valuables in the safe at your hotel." He also suggested that I never buy weed from the Rastafarian with two gold front teeth because it was usually crushed oregano!

After eight hours that seemed like days, my long legs were agonizingly cramped and we hadn't stopped since the midpoint of the trip. I had to go to the bathroom extremely badly, and at the point of panic, just when I'd started thinking about urinating in a paper cup, we arrived at our destination. It was a Jamaican-style environment, smiling locals greeting people with a simple "Cool" or "Yeah Mon." I felt welcomed and safe as we walked down the street to the surf camp, and my friends were outside when I arrived. With my pale white skin and bright blue eyes, I looked like a salamander that had just come out from under his rock. They were surprised to see me and gave me high-fives, and immediately broke out some brown, flattened bud and rolled a thumb-sized joint. My friend who owned the hotel led me to my room, which was aptly named "The Rat's Nest," and I unpacked my belongings and set up my mosquito net, which I was told was a necessity. Unfortunately, I'd only been able to find one that tented my upper body, with a net blanket for my legs. I figured that this would be fine and drifted off into a deep sleep with the sound of waves crashing in the background.

   I dreamt of scantily clad women on a palm tree-lined white beach bordering perfect waves. I grudgingly awoke to a hard knock on my door and my friend whispering, "Man, it's going off! I just checked the waves from the sky deck and it's double overhead and glassy!" This was enough to excite any real surfer, and I got out of bed in the early light to go for my first surf session in Paradise. I turned on the bedroom light and was shocked to see dozens of bright red bumps on my legs. Apparently the mosquito net hadn't worked too well; mosquitoes had unmercifully attacked my glowing white body and feasted on my fresh gringo blood. It didn't bother me, though; my heart was racing with the earth-rumbling sound of waves breaking in the distance, and I ran down the dirt street to the place where we'd paddle out.

I could barely make out the waves when we arrived at the beach, as it was only the crack of dawn. We sat under a banyan tree with twisted branches and shiny, green leaves and waxed our surfboards. One of my friends explained the treacherous paddle out to the surf zone inches above razor-sharp reef, and the narrow channel you could escape through if you happened to get caught inside. I was tentative as I watched him jump into the ocean, where he was pulled quickly through the opening in the reef and disappeared into the large, dark bumps of water on the horizon. The orange sun was just starting to rise as I delicately walked over the jagged reef to the water's edge. My stomach was in turmoil, and I took full breaths to center myself as I waded into the channel and was immediately swept away like a stick in a gutter after a rainstorm.

Someone screamed: the sound of being either thrown over the falls of a wave or engulfed in a giant tube, followed by the explosion of water on reef. As I paddled into the takeoff zone, I saw someone get spit out of a cylindrical barrel. He screamed again, claiming his ride like a soccer player after he makes a goal. I had adrenaline pumping through my veins, and I paddled fast and hard for the horizon as a gigantic set of waves loomed in the distance. I seemed to be far enough outside and in the right spot, so I instinctively paddled into the first wave of the set, only to get hung up in the lip and pulled backward over the falls into the abyss. I'll never forget the feeling of horror as I dropped into the gigantic wave and waited to be thrown into the exposed reef. Luckily, the wave broke before I impacted the bottom, and the white water lifted me back up into the air, where I took a quick breath before being churned through the washing cycle of ocean turbulence. After using up my lungs' air supply, I frantically swam to the surface; my board had been ripped from my grasp underwater. I gasped and choked for air as I surfaced, only to see another ominous wave about to break on my head. Thankfully, I had learned to surf in the large, cold waves of Northern California, and from experience I knew to relax, conserve my energy, and wait for the set to subside. Finally, it did just that, and I was relieved to see that my board wasn't broken and my leash was still attached to it. My friends hollered for me to paddle hard because another set was coming, so I gathered all of the energy I could to narrowly escape another beating. I sat outside the waves in deeper water to catch my breath from the thrashing I had taken, and my friends smiled from ear to ear as they paddled back out, reliving their last rides.

After I had recovered, I paddled into a midsize wave to test my skills again. This time it was a smooth takeoff, but the wave doubled in size as it hit the reef. There was nothing I could do but go straight into the eye of the beast, and the wave broke and enclosed me in a perfect green room of water. It's something that is hard to describe, being inside of a wave as it breaks over a coral reef a few feet beneath you. One wrong move could mean disaster, and truly only a surfer knows this incredible feeling. I felt spray hit me in the back, and a friend shouted as I flew out of the cave of water and into the sunlight. It was a feeling of sheer ecstasy; now I had been initiated into the tropical surf environment. This was symbolic of rebirth, and it heralded a new chapter in my life.

The following months were filled with daily surf trips, all-night partying, and enough rice and beans for a lifetime. We played softball with the locals, Rastas vs. the Gringos, and bonded with our new friends by smoking the international aloha. After a few months, I decided to travel over to the Pacific side of the country with a few friends who had an open spot in their rent-a-car. We drove all night and day, across the small country bordered by two oceans, and ended up in another small town on the Pacific side. There were only a hotel and a few bars and restaurants at the end of the cul-de-sac, but one of my friends and I found lodging in the spare room of a family's house. A multicolored parrot made its home in the tree outside our window, and a myriad of jungle creatures, from iguanas to monkeys, would parade by throughout the day. There was also a French bakery with mouth-watering cakes and buttery croissants, and strong espresso that made you sweat profusely in the tropical setting.

Traveling: The School of Life

I met another friend who was there with his family, and we traveled to a secret surf spot a few hours south over a bumpy, pothole-ridden road. To access the beach, we had to park by a creek where monkeys played in the trees and walk down a trail with wispy tall grass on either side. The effort was well worth it when we made it to the beach and surveyed the perfect waves devoid of surfers. We surfed for hours, and we came back to that same location day after day. I fell in love with this area that seemed to be lost in time, where there was no electricity, telephones, or services of any kind. The authentically friendly locals would stand outside of their tin houses and smile and wave as we sped by in our four-wheel-drive minibus, unwittingly creating a dust storm in our wake. It gave me a strange but warm feeling to see the locals so happy even though they seemed to live in poverty. However, I had a lot to learn about the world, and I was jaded from growing up in the land of abundance, where happiness was determined by material possessions, success, and pleasurable pursuits.

This first journey to a third-world country awakened me to the fact that external sources don't bring lasting fulfillment. Most Americans spent their lives working a dreadful nine-to-five existence in the pursuit of a nice house, a car, and wealth, and the majority were unhappy, depressed, and searching for contentment and peace of mind in their fast-paced lives. I wondered how the inhabitants of the jungle towns I had visited were so happy, the friendliest people I had ever met, even though they were so poor materially. It seemed like they were living a good, family-oriented life in their natural habitat, in harmony and flow with the seasons. I now questioned what true happiness was, and what would give me contentment and everlasting joy in this lifetime. A shift of awareness had occurred that allowed me to see how I had been conditioned by the society and small-town mentality I'd grown up in: to think that material things and external factors of momentary happiness were the recipe for joy and contentment.

I knew without a doubt that I had found my second home, and that I'd be returning to the jungle oasis many times in the years to follow. I had found an escape from civilization as I knew it, and I'd enjoy many tropical surfing vacations in the future, to rest and renew myself in the relaxing atmosphere, and to be in tune with nature and the elements. At the same time, being on the road helped me to appreciate the things that I took for granted at home. This was another step on my spiritual path, cultivating gratitude and appreciation for all of the blessings and gifts in my life and the cornucopia of opportunities in my eclectic hometown. Traveling had already opened my eyes to different realities of life, and I would travel on to new countries and cultures for more priceless schooling in the quest for happiness.

European Vacation

I had always wanted to go to Europe to visit the home of my ancestors. Being a North American of mixed heritage, I had no cultural identity, but I still had a desire to travel to the place of my forefathers. I was becoming an insatiable world traveler, and I planned to visit Western Europe to surf the famed beaches of southern France and of Portugal, the birthplace of my great-grandparents. This was a completely different excursion than going to Latin America; I had the burning desire to travel the world and explore as many countries and cultures as I could after that amazing journey.

My first stop was Amsterdam, Holland, where I would stay for a few weeks, and I booked lodging in advance at a local youth hostel. Having a fondness for marijuana definitely set my course for "Sin City," where marijuana was basically legal and you could order it in certain cafes. After I arrived at the airport I took the fast train into the city; I gazed out the window at the Dutch architecture, storybook windmills setting the scene. I had reached my destination at last, and it was as if I had landed on another planet. I squeezed out of the train, carrying my heavy backpack with cushion-less straps that dug into my bony shoulders. I also had a seven-foot-long bag filled with two surfboards and surfing accessories. Walking out of Central Station into the medieval city, I knew that I had definitely arrived at a place beyond my imagination, where many exciting events would unfold.

I found my lodging amid the maze of streets and Gothic buildings and checked into the youth hostel, which accommodated ten people per floor, with shared bathrooms. The stairs were steep and slippery, and with my awkward bags, it took me a long time to reach the fifth floor. Smiling people were milling around, and I was surprised by all of the friendly hellos and inquiries as to where I was from. After talking with a few people and eating a communal dinner, I decided to stroll through the city in search of one of the famed cannabis cafes.

It was freezing cold outside as I made my way through the narrow canal streets laid in red brick. They were lined with Renaissance-style architecture, each building connected to the next, with its own unique rooftop adornment or statues to differentiate one from the other. As

I was walking down a dark, unlit side street, I realized that I might be lost. Suddenly, a ghostly figure jumped out at me from behind a stairwell. He had a sharp needle in his hand.

"I'll stick you with this if you don't give me some money," he hissed in a gravelly voice. In shock, I reached into my pocket and handed him a few dollars, but purposely dropped it as he grabbed for it with his dirt-stained hand. As he bent over to pick up the money, I ran down the corridor toward a distant area where bright red lights shone from all of the windows.

Out of danger, taking a few deep breaths while surveying my surroundings, I wondered, "Is this the famous Red Light District of Amsterdam?" I walked up to the first window with neon-red lighting, and inside on a wooden stool sat an unbelievably beautiful woman in revealing lingerie. Our eyes connected and she beckoned me inside with a wiggle of her finger and a sensuous smile and lick of her lustrous pink lips. Being shy and reserved, I only gave a polite wave and strolled by. I passed an assortment of windows occupied by women of all shapes and sizes, and some establishments had dozens of foreign men giggling and looking in at the women of the night. At one location, three drunken Asian men were pushing a friend into the doorway as he tried to run away. They managed to get him through the door, and then they ran back to the window to see if they could get a peek at the happenings inside. Within minutes the unwilling friend ran out, and they tackled each other, laughing. I could tell from his body language that he was describing his short-lived encounter.

I came upon a colorful district where cannabis cafes lined the boulevards, with different themes and names like Blues Brothers, The Green House, and Rolling Stone. I entered one of the many and was greeted by a buxom, blonde barmaid who escorted me to an upstairs table beside stained-glass windows overlooking the street. She handed me a bulky menu, and I opened it to reveal actual sample packages of bud and hashish. Coming from the draconian laws of the States, where you were treated as a criminal for possessing even a little bit of marijuana, I was blown away by the liberal and accepting atmosphere I found myself in. I ordered my favorite strain, named Bubblegum because of its abundance of crystals, and a foamy Dutch beer as people rolled cone-shaped joints around me. I was curious as to how and why they were rolling such huge cylindrical reefers, and I asked the waitress what they were doing. She informed me that they were rolling tobacco mixed with cannabis, and that not many locals rolled pure bud joints. "They think that you Americans are crazy," she said with a smile. She set down a silver tray with rolling papers and my chosen bud and beer, and left with a polite "Enjoy." I was in cannabis heaven as I rolled up my own big joint and smoked it inside of a bar, legally for the first time in my life.

Whether from the jet lag, the culture shock, or the powerful herb I had just smoked, I started to get a little anxious about my environment. I could see in my periphery that there was a tall man holding a beer and staring at me. I was too stoned and paranoid to turn around, so I sat there wondering why I was the focus of this man's attention. It seemed like time stood still as I waited for him to leave or turn away, yet he continued to stand there watching my every move. I nervously asked for the check and paid so I could leave immediately. My plan was to go to the bathroom and then slip out if the mysterious man wasn't following me, but first I decided to briefly glance back at him as I stood up, to see who I was dealing with. I couldn't believe my eyes: It was a painted wood statue of a smiling sailor holding a beer mug! I laughed to myself and shook my head at the comedy of the delusion, and knew that my European vacation had truly begun.

I returned to the hostel and awoke the next morning to Queen's Day, Holland's annual three-day celebration. As it is the biggest holiday of the year, the streets were filled with thousands of people making their way through the narrow canal streets. I decided to venture out after breakfast. I melted into the crowd and started going with the flow of the tide of humans. People were laughing, screaming, shouting, and having a great time celebrating in the cold but sunny weather. It was like a stampede of raging bulls, and all too soon I was being swept away into a side street that looked too narrow for the hundreds of partygoers approaching it like ants going into their nest. I was crushed by people on all sides, and as we approached an intersection of two streets going into one tight corridor, the crowd slowed and I was lifted off the ground by the convergence of so many people. There was no way I could move, and now I was being pushed to the edge of the frenzy toward a sectioned-off area of an outdoor restaurant. Like a tidal surge, the sea of humans overtook the canal bistro, and I was rapidly approaching a table of eight people enjoying their brunch. I was fighting to avoid being pushed into them, but against my will I was thrown headfirst onto their table. I was on top of plates of deviled eggs and hot biscuits and gravy, and all I could do was quickly apologize and roll off the side of the table as others shared my fate. Besides swimming in the canal, there was no way to escape except to rejoin the human stew. I worked my way back into the crowd and traveled with it through street after street, passing theatrical performances, concerts, and the biggest parties I'd seen in my life. I stopped for a few beers and to smoke some herb along the route, and throughout my wanderings I never had any idea what part of the city I was in. I was just lost, drunk, stoned, and completely overwhelmed by my first few days in Europe. Somehow I made it back to the youth hostel the next day on autopilot and fell asleep instantly, exhausted from being up all night.

   In the days that followed, I explored the country outside of Amsterdam on a rented bicycle. Most of the locals in the country ride bicycles, whereas the city has a modern transportation system of trams and trains for wherever you need to go. The countryside was filled with blooming flowers and scenery straight out of a Van Gogh painting, and it was nice to get a different perspective. Back in the

European Vacation

city, I went to various art museums and the fabled Anne Frank house, which made me sadly aware of the hell that she and other Jewish people suffered in World War II. The city was bursting with history and energy, and I felt a connection with the surroundings and the liberal environment. I made some friends from other countries, and we enjoyed going to clubs and cafes, experimenting with pot brownies and cannabis cakes that left you in a state of unconsciousness. I was indulging to the extreme in marijuana-related substances, but there came a point where I knew that I needed to get out of there for my sanity. I was just starting to learn, through trial and error, that moderation is the best policy regarding the mind-altering plant.

After my wild adventure in Amsterdam, I took a train to Paris. The conductor scoffed as I squeezed my seven-foot surfboard bag through the doors and set it down in front of him. "You cannot put that bag there, Monsieur!" he dramatically informed me in English with a thick French accent, his hands in the air.

"Where can I put it?" I questioned politely.

"You must buy a sleeping cabin ticket for you and your oversized luggage," he said in an irritated tone, eyes bulging. A sleeper cabin would cost three times as much, but I had no desire to argue with the angry Frenchman, so I paid him the fare.

The night train is great for long-distance travel, as you can sleep away hours of the journey and arrive at your destination the next morning well rested. I arrived in the famed city of Paris and needed to catch a connection to the southern beach town of Biarritz at another train station. I planned to stay there for a few weeks and surf some of the famous beach breaks in the surrounding area. I only spoke the common phrases in French, and when I tried to ask people for directions to the next train station, they either ignored me or pointed and said something I didn't understand. I drifted through the city streets with a confusing map that I had bought, but after a few hours I knew I had gone the wrong direction. I sat down on a bench in the morning mist, admiring the statues and works of art that seemed to be everywhere. To my disbelief, out of the fog emerged a figure carrying a surfboard, and I walked toward him with a friendly "Bonjour!" "Aye, mate, are you an American? I can spot 'em from a mile away," he joked with a British accent. I informed him of my quandary, and he invited me to come with him, as he was taking the train to southern France as well. On the way, we talked and became friends, and he said that he had a flat near the beach where I could stay for a few nights! Traveler's luck had struck, and my journey headed down a new course thanks to my fortunate meeting with a fellow surfer.

During my stay with him, we surfed every day in the perfect sand-bottomed waves in the Bay of Biscay, and lounged on the gorgeous beaches eating baguettes with cheese while enjoying laughter and good conversation. I departed after two weeks; I might have overstayed my welcome, but he was so polite and hospitable that I extended my time in his abode. He had treated me as a good friend and given me valuable information about traveling in Europe, and I felt lucky to have stumbled upon the situation. He directed me to the train station where I would depart for Spain and Portugal, and I set off on foot with my oversize surfboard bag and backpack. On the hour-long walk through the vibrant French countryside, I thought about how the challenges of my youth were a distant memory, and I would be able to create a new life for myself by becoming a man of virtue. I had no idea that the next leg of my journey would steer me on a course that would change my perspective on life forever, and show me more unbelievable hospitality from strangers in a foreign land.

I took the train to Madrid for a one-night layover before heading to Lisbon, Portugal, the next day. I made the mistake of boarding a transit bus in front of an older Spanish woman, who began yelling and trying to pull me off the stairs of the bus. Apparently, I had been disrespectful by getting on in front of her, even though she'd been twenty feet away when I stepped onto the first step. She shouted in Spanish to the bus's occupants that a stinking gringo had pushed her out of the way in line. I received surprised stares and mumblings of displeasure from those around me, and learned a bit of travelers' etiquette: Have the utmost respect for elders while on the road. Sometimes you have to learn the rules and manners of foreign countries through experience, and unexpected scenarios happen all the time, no matter how aware you are of your surroundings.

I spent the night in a shanty hostel in central Madrid with other weary budget travelers and awoke early the next morning to return to the central station for my train to Lisbon. I was a sight to see in the center of the city, walking with my giant, blue surfboard bag through the crowded business district. Curios locals asked me what I was carrying. I just smiled, feeling like my life was a blank canvas and I was painting on it with every footstep.

  Once there, I encountered another problem with my oversized bags: I was told that I would have to leave them in the cargo compartment behind my sleeper cabin for the twelve-hour passage on the night train. I unenthusiastically complied and handed my board bag over to a smiling baggage handler. He said, "No problema, amigo" when I asked if the boards would be safe in the cargo hold, which was a separate car behind my sleeper cabin. Assured that my possessions would be safe, I entered the train and located my bunk to lie down for the long ride to the country of my great-grandparents.

The Mysterious Woman Who Saved My Surf Trip

    I awoke to a gentle shaking of the cabin as the train came to a screeching halt. I had slept through the entire ride from Madrid, and I felt refreshed and re-energized. I gathered the belongings that I never let out of my sight—passport, traveler's checks, and emergency contact numbers—and stepped off of the train into Portugal. I looked around at the centuries-old train station's high ceilings and shadowy ambiance, realizing that I had to retrieve my surfboard bag from the cargo car. To my bewilderment, I saw that my sleeper cabin was the last part of the train, and the cargo cars that had been behind it were no longer attached! I anxiously ran up to someone and asked him what had happened to the cargo cars that had formed the back half of the train. He mumbled that he didn't speak English and waved me off with a flick of his wrist. I frantically ran around the station asking everyone if they spoke English. Then I heard the piercing sound of a train whistle. The train I had been on was leaving without any explanation, and I stood there in shock as it sped away into the distance. I couldn't believe it: All of my clothes, shoes, surfboards, and travel accessories were now lost. Luckily, I had my

The Mysterious Woman Who Saved My Surf Trip

important documents and money, but surfing gear and clothes were expensive in Europe, and I knew that my surf trip would be cut very short.

I sat down on a bench beneath a scowling gargoyle and tried to figure out what I was going to do next. I decided to go talk to the station conductor. I walked into his office and was met with the same response: He didn't speak English. He was quite annoyed by my desperate communication effort and pointed to the door for me to leave. Just then, the door opened and a smiling older woman walked in. As I pleaded one more time with the conductor, the woman interjected, "I can help you translate, I speak some English." A guiding angel with impeccable timing had walked into the office, and I related my story to her. She spoke to the conductor in Portuguese, and his frown changed to a look of understanding. He picked up the phone, and a few minutes later he looked up at us and smiled and said something to the woman.

"Ah, your bags were left at the Spain/Portugal border in the middle of the night because you didn't have proper documentation on them," she told me. She also informed me that it was about a twelve-hour drive in a car to the border, and that I couldn't take a train because there was no stop there, only a rural outpost station where they checked bags for documentation. "Come with me and I'll make you lunch and we will try to figure this out," she said, extending her help even more. She was a petite older woman who looked harmless and had a nice energy about her, so I accepted her generous offer, and we walked out into the city together to hail a taxi.

In the backseat of the taxi, I told her a little about my life and my reasons for coming to Europe, and Portugal in particular. My great-grandparents were from Portugal and my great-grandma had grown up in the small beach town of Peniche, which also had one of the best surf spots in the country. The woman listened and laughed at my stories, and I learned quickly that she was very positive, with something nice to say about everything.

We arrived at the modest flat where she lived with one of her daughters and her German husband. There were other family members and friends inside when I arrived, and they immediately took me in, treating me like one of their own. I was fed until I had to decline any more food, an endless succession of delicious courses presented on the long kitchen table. We also shared bottles of local wine, and they boasted about the region where it was grown and other facts about their country. It was interesting to hear about part of my cultural background. The day finally caught up with me, and my eyelids drooped like heavy curtains at the end of a play, slowly closing after a dramatic scene. I vaguely remember being led to a dimly lit room and sliding under the sheets of a warm, comfortable bed where I felt safe and at home, and I fell into a dreamless slumber.

I awoke late the next afternoon. Everyone was gathered again in the living room, sharing food and conversation. They were delighted to see me and wanted to hear more about my life and American traditions. After a strong cup of coffee I felt more social, but finding the board bag containing most of my belongings and my beloved surfboards was my main objective. I asked the kind woman who'd befriended me at the train station if she knew anything more about the whereabouts of my stuff. With a big smile she said, "Why yes, I talked to the conductor again and apparently your bags are safe and waiting to be picked up." I was elated to hear this, and she insisted that since I didn't know the country, her son-in-law and daughter would drive me to the outpost. I couldn't believe this kindness, and I wondered why she was helping me so much. But as a traveler in need, I accepted her offer, and we took off that evening for our long drive to the remote outpost.

The drive was enjoyable thanks to lively conversation, and the hours spent winding through the lush countryside went by quickly. They wanted to drive all night and do a twenty-four-hour round trip where we all took turns at the wheel, which was fine by me. After a full day of driving, we entered an area that looked like a desert, and we stopped to get gas in a small ghost town where sand whipped into the air and tumbleweeds danced across the dirt streets. The gas station attendant pointed to a mountain off in the distance and spoke to us in Portuguese. They translated that we were close to the border station, and to head toward the mountains on this road.

About an hour down a bumpy road, it seemed like we were in a maze that we couldn't get out of, and it started to get dark and the outpost was nowhere in sight. We finally spotted a little wooden shack; after we drove over the railroad tracks, we realized that we had found our destination. The outpost looked like an outhouse, with a flickering oil lantern that added to the dreariness of the setting. I laughed sarcastically and said there was no way that my seven-foot board bag was inside that wooden box. We parked close to it and a man in a weathered uniform materialized from the darkness. My companions greeted him and explained our story in their native tongue, and with a dry, wheezing laugh that reeked of alcohol and cigarettes, he led us to the door of the outpost. He opened it up. To my absolute disbelief, there was my board bag in the corner of the shack! I threw a fist into the air and screamed like a child opening his Christmas presents as I looked into the bag and saw that my surfboards and valuables were all inside and unharmed. We strapped the board bag onto the top of the car, and I gave the outpost serviceman a generous tip. He seemed very pleased and shook my hand with both of his in a silent gesture of appreciation. As we drove away, leaving him in his rocking chair, I thanked the powers that be for the return of my possessions so that I could continue my journey as planned, and for the kind family that had befriended me.

Upon our return to their house, they refused any money for gas or food, even though it had been a full day of driving and they had treated me to many meals. We had another big party with plenty of food, laughter, and wine, and it was heartwarming to be a part of their family tradition of gatherings, celebrating life each and every day as if it were the last.

The next day, I was eager to resume my trip to the coast and the beach city where my great-grandmother had spent most of her youth. The family gathered and wished me well and gave me gifts for the road. I choked up in gratitude and thanked all of them for treating me with such warmth and generosity. The kind woman who'd saved my surf trip after our fateful meeting in the train station took me aside and said, "I have one last story to tell you."

She told me that one of her daughters had been robbed in Brazil years ago. Left with nothing but the clothes on her back, she'd begged in the streets for someone to help her. A compassionate woman took her in and paid for her ticket home to Portugal, and asked for nothing in return. She'd said only that she was passing on the help that someone else had offered her when she was stranded in a foreign country, and that if she could pass this gift on to someone else, then the chain of generosity would remain unbroken. "This is what I'm passing on to you now," my friend conveyed to me with open arms, "and if you get the chance to help someone in need, then please do so to keep the cycle going." I pondered her words as I waved goodbye to the friends I had made, and I walked on with my backpack and recovered surfboard bag down the road to another horizon. I knew that my life had been changed forever by their unconditional kindness; it was an experience that I would cherish in my heart forever.

In the years that followed, I dedicated myself even more to being a generous person and friend to all people, and to help those in need in whatever way I could. These random acts of kindness would become a part of my daily routine, giving me a sense of contentment I had never felt in my life. And embedded in my heart and memory is the beautiful family in a foreign country who taught me the greatest of lessons: to be of service to others in need, and to treat every person with respect, compassion, and consideration on their own unique journey.

There is an intrinsic joy that comes with the path of service to mankind, for by helping others, we help ourselves find peace, meaning, and fulfillment in our own lives. Many spiritual traditions hold that all beings are connected by a common thread: the divine creator that sees and experiences life through us. I now understood that by giving without expecting something in return, I would open the door to the same treatment from others and experience lasting contentment. By choosing to be a happy, respectful, and optimistic person, I was encountering the same in other people everywhere I went.

Traveling through Europe added another piece to the puzzle of my happiness and growth as an individual, and I returned home months later with more self-confidence, patience, compassion, and humility, among other positive attributes. Traveling to distant lands was a chance to start over again, becoming wiser and more capable of living a better life by changing my perspective and attitude and realizing that happiness is a choice. I was being guided by unseen forces, pulled toward my destiny by a sea of external circumstances, and there were many more lessons to be learned as I returned home a different man.

A Life Cut Short

A tornado of pain once more descended on my peaceful existence. I was jolted awake in the middle of the night by desperate knocking on the sliding glass door of the studio I rented, down the street from the ocean. Groggy and not feeling well from partying the night before, I yelled, "Go away." The knocking became more frantic, and I got out of bed to see who was bothering me at such a late hour. It was my white-haired friend's girlfriend, and she had tears streaming down her face. She asked me if she could come in. "What's going on?" I asked with a trace of anxiety.

"He's dead. He died last night at one a.m.," she cried as she wrapped her arms around me and wept uncontrollably. She didn't have to say it again. I felt a wave of grief encompass my heart and soul.

"How did he die, what happened?" I asked as she poured tears onto my shoulder.

"He had a heart attack in his sleep. I woke up to him gasping for air and unconscious. I called 911. When the paramedics arrived they couldn't resuscitate him, and he was pronounced dead at the hospital," she managed to say through sobs and gasps.

I consoled her until she left to break the news to family and other friends. My mind was blank, and I couldn't comprehend what was going on; I had just hung out with my friend yesterday and he'd seemed fine. I called my brother and left a grief-stricken message about the death of our mutual friend. I had no idea that while I left the message, my brother was lying in bed wide awake, thinking about a dream he had just awoken from, in which our friend who'd died had appeared. In the dreamscape our friend was in a fearful, anxious condition, asking my brother a myriad of questions. A chill ran up my brother's spine when he awoke in the morning; he was thinking, "Wow, what an intense dream" at the moment I called weeping to leave a message about our friend's death. My brother was deep into meditation and spiritual practices at that time, and he was probably the only person with whom our friend could commune in the afterlife. He later described the meeting as "a thousand questions and answers in a few moments, but by the end of the soul-to-soul communication our departed friend was in a better state of consciousness."

In disbelief, I passed out in my sleeping loft, telling myself that it was all just a dream, a crazy nightmare in

A Life Cut Short

which my soul brother, my closest friend and ally, had died unexpectedly in a mysterious way. When I woke up the next day, still hung over from the night before, I convinced myself that it really had been just a bad dream. I started to believe myself, until I saw my friend's brother approaching my door with tears in his eyes. I collapsed, faint from the realization that it was true; he was dead, and I would grieve his death for years to come, as would his family, his friends, and the entire surfing community.

The close-knit surf town came together to mourn their lost friend, the man everyone knew as one of the most popular character in the Northern California surf scene. Hundreds of people paddled out into the ocean to scatter my friend's ashes over his brothers. They let out a primal scream, igniting all of the friends and acquaintances, united in a circle in the ocean, to join the chorus. There were thousands of onlookers gathered on the cliffs for this media-publicized event, and it was said that the sound of the screams echoed for miles. We gave each other solemn looks and nods and disbanded, and the multitude of surfers paddled into the lineup and caught waves together in his honor. I paddled away and didn't have the energy to stand up as a wave gently pushed me to shore. The comfort of being on my surfboard in the turbulent whitewater was all that I wanted, and I felt in my heart that my deceased friend would always be with me, and one day we would meet again on another plane of existence.

As I walked up the beach and looked out over the crystal blue ocean with my surfboard under my arm, I remembered my friend saying, a couple of days before he died, that he had been sitting on the cliff and thinking about death. He had confided in me that he wasn't afraid to die, and that he saw it as a peaceful transition to another reality. It was as though he'd had a premonition of his untimely death. I thought about how his passing on was teaching me to live life to its fullest every moment, as you never know when your time is up. And to not fear death, but to see it as the only inevitable conclusion and transition of our consciousness, and to make peace with that truth. As I reminisced and contemplated life, a dolphin jumped into the air in a playful display, and this would become the symbol that I would engrave on my shoulder as a memorial to our sacred friendship.

Death confronts all of us at some point, and it's the greatest of mysteries, for although there is speculation, there is no solid evidence as to what happens after we leave our bodies. We can look to literature such as *The Tibetan Book of the Dead,* a book on the science of death, which offers insight into what may confront us as we pass through the "between" states of consciousness in the afterlife. This Eastern culture's narratives and teachings on death have comforted me in times when I felt death was stalking me, or when I've been confronted with the passing of a close friend or relative. Our delicate lives come and go on the earth's landscape like statues disintegrating in the dust of time. Many religions and spiritual teachings suggest that we accept and embrace the impermanence of our existence in this world, and that our soul is eternal and after we die, it lives on in a different realm of consciousness. My brother's visitation in his dream, from our friend who had died, was a testament to this concept. By accepting this, we don't resist the inevitable and can prepare for this transition, and we can walk through death's doorway without fear but, rather, with awareness and acceptance. I hoped that my friend's revelation before he died had put him in this state of acceptance as he transitioned between realities, and I felt in my heart that his powerful spirit would live eternally.

The Guardian Angel Invoked

I was an emotional wreck for the months that followed my friend's sudden death, and I hung out with other close friends as I tried to absorb what had happened. But now I felt that my white-haired friend was my guardian angel living through me; this made me feel at peace and gave me strength to move on with my own life. The spiritual principles of acceptance and non-attachment were concepts that I was just beginning to learn and conceptualize after reading a Buddhist text that explained their meanings. According to the principle of non-attachment, the more we're attached to people, places, and material objects, the more we suffer in our lives. And acceptance of what happens in our lives allows us to move on from sadness, anger, guilt, or other emotions that can cause us suffering. These are invaluable concepts that helped me to cope with losing someone so close to me.

One evening, a group of us met up to go to a party in honor of our deceased friend. We were already drunk before we left the house, so we decided to ride bicycles to be safe. In a small beach town you can do this: jump on your beach cruiser and glide toward the house parties and local get-togethers without running into neighborhood traffic. We drank and socialized in our own neanderthal way until two a.m., then jumped on our bikes for the short ride back to home base. We swerved in and out of the streets in the hours of darkness, a few of us riding on handlebars, the silence only broken by our chants to our departed friend.

Out of the darkness, bright headlights beamed on us, accompanied by hollers from a friend who had chosen to drive back from the gathering. "Jump in and I'll drive you guys home," he offered. Most of us were too drunk to talk or consider options, and with a few "woo-hoos," we stacked our bikes in the back of his jacked-up four-wheel-drive truck and took off. Including the driver, there were four people crowded into the front of the cab, and there were seven more of us in the back with eight bicycles between us. The ones in front rolled a fat joint and passed it back through the sliding window to the delight of the drunken crew, and we sped along our local route, back to where most of us lived or would be doing the couch tour.

The Guardian Angel Invoked

The truck suddenly took a sharp turn down a side street that I knew was a dead end. The driver was accelerating rapidly. I was in the back right corner of the vehicle, holding onto the side of the pickup for dear life and screaming for him to slow down. With a loud screech of the tires, he pulled the emergency brake, sending the truck into an uncontrolled skid so that we almost rolled over. Some were so inebriated that they were laughing with delight and shouting words of approval, but when we momentarily stopped after the E-brake slide, I yelled for him to let me out. Like a roller coaster, the car sped toward the wall of a building, and the driver pulled the E-brake again. I tried to free my legs from underneath the bicycles and jump out, but I was hopelessly trapped as everything went into slow motion. The truck slid and tipped over onto its side, and I made the split-second decision to pull my arm in from outside the bed; if I hadn't, it would have been crushed by the weight of the vehicle. The side of my face hit the cement first, and then, as the truck jumped into the air, along with its eleven occupants and multiple bicycles, I was ejected onto my hip, landing with a thud ten feet away. I'll never forget the sound of metal crushing and screeching across the asphalt, and then the silence as the truck rolled over onto its opposite side. The unlucky occupants were scattered near and far, and the ones in the cab let out moans and cries of pain as they came to their senses. A few had been miraculously thrown from the back without suffering any injuries, and they were yelling in shock and bewilderment. I had crawled over to a nearby wall, and my body convulsed in pain. Blood was pouring from a deep cut above my eye and the right side of my face had been smashed into the cement upon impact. My entire right arm was shredded with lacerations, and skin had scraped off of my hand and knuckles; to add to the injuries, my hip had a pancake-size piece of skin missing. I knew that I was hurt bad, and I was starting to pass out from all of the combined pain and trauma.

Amazingly, all of the others had survived with minor cuts and abrasions, except one who needed stitches on his lip from hitting the dashboard. I had crawled far away, and when they saw me writhing in pain, they all came running over. I remember voices saying, "He's hurt bad," and "We need to take him to the hospital." One uninjured comrade jumped on his bicycle to go call 911 or to hail a ride for me. A passerby in a car stopped and gave me a ride to the hospital, where I was patched up with sixteen stitches above my eye and had gravel picked out of my numerous cuts, bruises, and lacerations. When I finally made it home and looked in the mirror to see a swollen face and a deep gash above my right eye, I couldn't believe that the evening had turned into such a disaster. I was thankful to be alive and without serious injuries or broken bones, and I felt that our white-haired friend had been our guardian angel in the nightmarish accident. How else could so many people have gone relatively uninjured in such a freak accident?

Sometimes events are beyond our control; for some unknown reason, we're put through the most challenging of situations, which cause us pain and suffering. The driver of the vehicle was just trying to have fun and had no intention of hurting himself or his friends, but it took me a long time to see the situation for what it was: an ignorant, alcohol-infused event that had disastrous consequences. This is when I made the conscious decision to stop drinking and doing hard drugs, because they had only caused me misery and made me act like someone I wasn't. The taste of alcohol had never agreed with me, and I had only drunk it to become intoxicated; this usually involved a drama of some sort for me or for those in the same condition. This was the bright side of the experience; I realized what wasn't serving me anymore, and how to forgive and have

The Guardian Angel Invoked

compassion for what happens in my life. Through forgiveness and acceptance of the past, I moved on from this incident; part of acceptance is believing that everything happens for a reason, which is a comforting blanket when disasters take place in our lives.

The Path of Yoga

As time rolled on and I left the party scene behind me in the shadows of the past, I became more serious about school, spirituality, nutrition, and taking care of my physical health. Even though I was reading and learning about various traditions of spiritual disciplines and practices, I was still, and always had been, living in the stressful environment of my mind. My brother was an experienced yoga practitioner, and he informed me as to how practicing yoga could help me to stop identifying with my mind (ego). He also explained that by bringing awareness to the body through yoga postures (asanas) and breath work (pranayama), I could live with more peace and inner silence in the eternal present moment. I was intrigued by this new paradigm of practicing awareness through movement and regulation of the breath, thus breaking the cycle of living in the mind's endless stream of chatter.

I decided to explore this discipline and registered for a Hatha yoga class three days a week. I had never known such pain and soreness as I attempted the various physical postures and movements, and I was unable to concentrate on the spiritual aspect of the practice because of the discomfort. As I found out much later, the science of yoga was working its way into my life; at the time, I was oblivious to the energetic power of the movements and the fact that I'd taken my first step in a new sadhana (spiritual practice).

After a few weeks of practicing the challenging postures, I started to notice that my surfing was progressing and that I was more flexible and felt stronger. I also became aware of an increase in my energy and clarity in school, as my yoga class took place early in the morning, before other academic courses. I had a permanent smile on my face, and for the first time I truly felt alive and energized all day long. The magic of the asanas was taking effect in a dramatic way, but it would take me a while to connect the practice of yoga to the vitality that I was feeling. After the semester ended, I continued to do yoga as a warmup for surfing, but without the guidance of an experienced teacher I didn't push myself to do such intense workouts. For many years I just explored the discipline, taking a few classes here and there but mainly practicing at home.

The Path of Yoga

It wasn't until another horrific accident that I became more knowledgeable about the spiritual side of yoga: the union between mind, body, and spirit. The accident and new teachings would change my life in drastic ways, projecting me onto a path I had never imagined. The path of yoga would now guide me through the inevitable hills and valleys of life on my journey of self-discovery. It would teach me things that I couldn't have learned in school or my social environment, and in time, the ancient practices would come to my aid in all aspects of life.

The Kiss of Death in the Snow Park

We arrived in Utah, the state of Mormons and mountains of powdery snow, on a midwinter day, after weeks of planning our snowboarding vacation. There were eight of us, friends from home and surf brethren from opposite sides of town. It had recently snowed, so the mountains were covered with powder, and we were ready to hit the slopes. We arrived at the resort as it opened and were the first to jump on the ice-covered lifts to the cold, mountainous peaks.

My friends were all experienced snowboarders, and I was trying to keep up with their aerial antics, reckless considering that I had only been snowboarding for a few years. After a few seasons of snowboarding, I was finding joy in carving down steep slopes of feathery snow, flying off of ledges and ravines into the soft pillow landings. However, I wasn't experienced in the snow parks, where veteran snowboarders flung themselves into acrobatic flips and twists in the half-pipe and off of manmade jump ramps. Our crew was discussing going to the park; at first I shied away, intuiting that I was probably better off staying on the

The Kiss of Death in the Snow Park

slopes, in my element. But wanting to share in their excitement, I hesitantly followed, my heart beating rapidly and adrenaline pumping for what was to come.

One by one, our group entered the park and followed each other jump after jump. I was last in line and staying about fifty yards behind a friend. The first several ramps were tabletops, so no matter how much speed you obtained before you hit a ramp, it leveled off and you only received a few seconds of airtime. My friend in front of me stopped after a few disappointing runs, and we laughed about how boring the park was and discussed going back to the mountain. However, there was one last jump ramp on the horizon. The morning sun's rays had lit it up, giving it a mirage effect.

My friend took off toward the sunlit ramp, and I followed, gathering as much speed as possible and hoping to be launched into the air, high above the crowd of spectators and friends. My goggles were slightly fogged up but I knew that I was going fast, and that this time I was going to get some serious airtime. Seconds before I approached the ramp, I noticed that it wasn't a tabletop but a half-pipe with a beyond-vertical lip, and with not even time for a breath before I flew up and off of it, I knew that I was in big trouble. Somehow, I had the instinct to relax and leave my arms at my sides as I was flung upside down twenty feet into the air, above a portion of the park that was all sheet ice. I had never been upside down in the air before, and as I flew through the sky, I could see onlookers pointing at me and hear gasps of despair. Then the top of my head hit the frozen snow, which proceeded to impact my entire backside in a non-choreographed sequence that knocked me out instantly, and I slid lifelessly on the ice.

The next thing I remember is choking for air and seeing blurred visions run toward me. I couldn't breathe or feel my body, and my first thought was that I had broken my neck and was dying. With a feeling of relief, I caught my breath, but I lay as still as I could, slowly moving first my fingers and then my toes. "I'm OK," I thought. I knew that if I could move my fingers and toes, then the spinal cord wasn't completely severed, but I also knew that moving at all could cause more damage. The snow medics arrived seconds later and gave me oxygen, which made me feel immediately giddy and in high spirits. A friend who had seen the incident skidded to a stop near me, pale and with an incredulous look on his face. "I thought you were dead, man, are you all right?"

"Yeah, no worries," I giggled, intoxicated from the oxygen as I tried to push myself up. The medics gently grabbed me and lowered me back to the snow, reminding me that I might have a spinal cord injury and not to move a muscle.

I was taken off of the mountain on a stretcher pulled behind a sputtering snowmobile, and hundreds looked from rooftops and lift areas at the poor injured man who they thought had attempted an incredible back flip. I was taken to the hospital in excruciating pain, certain that my back and neck were injured. I almost passed out on the X-ray table as they turned me from side to side in uncomfortable positions. It turned out that I had three compressed vertebrae and a slight fracture in another vertebra near my neck, and my entire back, from my butt to my head, was red and bruised from the impact. The nurse was kind enough to give me a shot of morphine, and I was able to walk out of the hospital with the help of some friends, albeit with a suggestion to fly home immediately and get more tests and X-rays.

The Kiss of Death in the Snow Park

I drifted in and out of consciousness on the flight home, and as the morphine wore off I groaned in agony. After I made it home, I took pain pills to take the edge off of the throbbing and tenderness in my backside, and I had to sleep in a sitting position; the discomfort was so intense that I couldn't lie on my back, stomach, or sides. For the next three months, I had a nightly ritual of waking up at three a.m. and not being able to go back to sleep. I would turn on the TV and watch reruns of *The Tonight Show* and *Conan O'Brien* and smoke herb, which eased the pain and aided me in eventually falling back to sleep. This was a testament to the efficacy of marijuana as a relaxant, sleep aid, and serious pain reliever.

Months later, the joyous day came when I walked out of my house to the ocean for the first time; I knew I had escaped being paralyzed and was grateful beyond description for the chance to live a normal life without handicaps. It would take years of physical therapy to put my body back together so that I could be relatively pain free, but I was able to resume my athletic lifestyle in time. Since I had been practicing yoga before the accident, I began to dedicate myself to healing postures that increased my injured body's strength and flexibility, and to apply the mind-body connection to healing injuries with deep relaxation and meditation. The path of yoga was opening up before me, and I took it with gratitude and a newfound conviction.

Realizations in the Jungle

My training as a yoga teacher in balmy Central America came about indirectly, after I decided to take some acting classes. I was in my early thirties and at a point in my life where I wanted change, and the acting classes were a way to see if I still had the desire to pursue my dream of the past. I was challenged and humbled during improvisation classes, but after the completion of the course and with praise from my acting coach, I made plans to go to New York City and test my skills among the best actors in the most competitive environment. I would have never guessed that this undertaking would converge with the path of studying the 5,000-year-old art and science of yoga.

On the flight from San Francisco to New York, I read a popular book on acting that stated: "To become an actor you must either be insane, or have a burning passion for it." This quote planted the seed of discontent and inquiry in my mind; was this something that I really had a passion for? Was I ready for the challenges of this type of work again? I was looking for a new career and trying to utilize the talents that I had, but I wasn't sure if this pursuit was the answer. Nevertheless, I was still committed to giving it my best effort, because I knew that if I didn't follow through with what I started, I would never find purpose and meaning in my life.

The cold streets of New York in early winter numbed my senses, and the uncertainty of what I was doing set in after a few weeks of being there, when I caught one of the worst colds of my life. I lay in bed in my Manhattan apartment one morning, coughing painfully, questioning my existence, and deeply depressed about what I was doing with my life. I'd known right away, after the shallow, superficial meetings with agents and managers, that this wasn't my heart's calling, or something that I wanted to pursue again. Out of desolation, I decided to call a good friend and confidant who lived in Central America and ask for his advice. A year before, he had taken a life-changing, month-long yoga teacher training that highlighted the heart-based, spiritual side of yoga. He informed me that another training was starting in a few weeks, and it sounded exactly like what I needed: a spiritually inspired program that would help me gain insight into my life. I had a gut feeling that this was a rare opportunity, even though I'd be once again abandoning my acting career. I jumped out of bed with an energy that I hadn't had since I'd arrived, and raced to an Internet cafe to make my reservation for the course, which would begin a few weeks later.

This spontaneous decision would guide me on a new river of self-discovery and awaken the awareness of the divine being within. Although I didn't realize it, I was still being ruled by negative mind-states (ego), and the teachings I'd receive would give me tools for overcoming the hurdles to happiness. I packed my bags and waved the Big Apple goodbye as I left in a taxi for the airport. I was excited to be going to a place where the ocean and air were warm, and to start a new chapter in my life under the guidance of renowned spiritual teachers. Once again, the path of yoga was drawing me deeper into its esoteric teachings and practices.

I arrived in a small but growing beach town in tropical Latin America a few days before the month-long training began. I had secured a place to stay near the ocean, and the waves were perfect, with light offshore winds caressing the turquoise water. The weather was hot and humid, and the white sand beaches intensified the blistering heat. There was a comforting energy and the locals seemed friendly, so I melted into the environment and surfed all day on the

Realizations in the Jungle

palm tree-lined beaches. I had heard that the training was intense, and that I should be ready for ten to twelve hours a day of yoga practice and teaching methodology. I had been doing yoga for quite some time, so I felt confident in my ability to perform yoga postures, but nothing could have prepared me for what was to come and the drastic shift of awareness that I would undergo.

Our group met for an orientation in a high-ceilinged rancho with a palm-leaf roof. The directors of the center had a glowing energy about them, with smiles that warmed your heart and a combined presence that made you feel peaceful and at home. There were fifty-five students of all ages, shapes, and sizes, but I was one of only five men. I had never been in such a large gathering of the opposite sex, and I felt anxious as we went around the circle to introduce ourselves. I was tensing up, and when my turn came, my voice had a higher pitch than usual. This was one of the few times I'd speak in the weeks to come; I chose to be more of an observer because I'd always had a fear of speaking in front of large groups, let alone fifty women!

Our daily activity began when we arrived at the rancho at six a.m., as the howler monkeys' calls echoed through the jungle, for an hour and a half of yoga practice. I wasn't used to doing yoga so intensely and early in the morning, and I sweated excessively in the humid air as we twisted our bodies into challenging poses named after animals, saints, and sages. We were supposed to breathe through our noses and make a hissing sound in our throats, but I was greedily gasping for air through my mouth, in unrelenting pain from the new body positions.

As the first class ended, and I lay down on my sticky mat in a pool of sweat in the relaxation pose, I didn't know if I could do this all day, every day, for a month. I started thinking of an escape route. The teacher's melodic voice guided us into a deep relaxation, which calmed my active mind. And as we chanted "Om" for the finale, a restorative wave of collective energy engulfed me; suddenly, I knew that I was in the right place at the right time. Without thinking, only observing, I became hyperaware of my thoughts. A subtle awakening had occurred inside of me, a veil had been lifted, and I became aware of a witnessing presence that gazed out through my eyes. In the tradition of yoga, this seer inside all of us is said to be our soul, and it will reveal itself when you're ready and able to recognize it as your true nature.

Realizations in the Jungle

The following weeks were filled with awakenings of many sorts as our bodies and minds were cleansed through yoga asanas, breathing exercises, and the study of the sage Patanjali's yoga sutras, which are a science for the realization of our true nature. I embraced the teachings as I learned that yoga accepts all religions and belief systems and is rooted in individuality and one's own unique expression of life. I was intrigued by the philosophy of yoga, which I had studied and utilized for rehabilitation from injuries, and the program took me further into its teachings and practices. We learned about the eight branches of Ashtanga yoga, with social and personal ethical conduct at the forefront of the lessons; this was comparable to what I'd learned from other spiritual traditions. The experiential teachings were combined with reflective listening exercises with a partner, as well as small-group interaction, which opened my heart, and gradually I came to feel like I was part of a close-knit family. The directors shined love and pure acceptance onto each and every student and masterfully guided our inquiries and questions back to our own hearts. The heart, they explained, is where all is known and revealed. I had shut down my heart for so long that I found myself spontaneously crying at different points throughout the training. It was a release like none I'd ever known and was usually followed by a bout of laughter and blissful joy—a joy not based on any stimulus or material thing or possession, just a happiness to be here in the moment, enjoying and being grateful for this incredible human experience.

Friday nights were reserved for the *Satsangha* (gathering for the truth), the most important part of the training as far as the directors were concerned. This was to be a gathering of all of the students. Our teachers would lead us in chanting, and then invite us to speak about whatever we wanted in front of the group.

On our first Friday night meeting, I was open to chanting, but I didn't feel ready to speak into a microphone about my life and/or current experience. I was still very mystified, and the transformation I was going through had made me question all that I believed in. Basically, I was scared and self-conscious, the twin enemies that rob you of your ability to speak in front of others, and I felt anxious even thinking about talking to the group of women about the dreamlike experience I was having both in and out of class. Crying like I hadn't in years and then going into fits of laughter? Was I insane? I had no idea what was going on, except that I was being guided to access my inner experience and my heart's wisdom; this was unknown territory for me.

In unison, we sang replies to our teachers' chants. I was ignorant to what I'd feel while chanting the sacred songs in the ancient language of Sanskrit, never having done it because I thought it was only for crazy hippies. In harmony, our group chanted the same lyrics over and over, going faster with each verse: "Om, guru, Om, guru, Deva Deva. Aja Kay, Ananda Key Jay." I had another bizarre experience in which my body seemed to be on autopilot as I witnessed myself from a detached perspective. We chanted for about an hour in the humid evening's breath, and after we finished I felt a silence in my being that I had never felt before. The chanting had brought me to a space of timelessness, here in the present moment, and I felt as blissful as a Buddha.

But the spiritual basking was soon interrupted by our director's announcement that it was now an "open microphone" and whoever wanted to speak was free to do so. For a few minutes, not one of the fifty-five attendees dared to bare their feelings. Finally, one brave soul came up and broke the dam of fear. She explained how happy she was to be here and that this was exactly what she needed, as her mother had recently passed away. Another woman explained in a slow drawl that a year ago, she'd had a horrible accident, after which she wasn't expected to live a normal life. She had barely recovered, and she was cherishing every moment even though she wasn't physically able to do all of the asana flow. Her dramatic story and many others that night opened me up to compassion in a direct way, and showed me the unity between all human beings regardless of gender. I was now beginning to understand women in a deeper way, and this assisted me in rectifying long-buried negative issues with my mother.

Growing up in a male-oriented surf culture had led me to objectify women in the past, and I was learning in this supportive program to see women in a different light. The beauty that was shining forth from all the women gave me a new outlook on attractiveness. I was figuring out that inner beauty is far more attractive than outer beauty. And I enjoyed being in a feminine environment where emotions and feelings were expressed; I grew more in touch with my own feelings just by listening and observing.

Nevertheless, I had made an intimate connection with one of the other students; and in a small group, gossip was like wind blowing through the trees. After it became known, many women wouldn't say hello or talk to me, even if I was being genuinely friendly. I understood that most of them thought I was there just to get laid. However, I saw no reason why I shouldn't explore a relationship while at the training, until a few weeks later, when the woman I was seeing informed me that she had recently broken up with her boyfriend back home, AND she was going through a nasty divorce. I had already suffered from this type of situation many times in the past, and I saw now why I shouldn't have become emotionally involved: It was a mental distraction from the teachings.

By the last week of the program, I was accustomed to the vigorous yoga routines and was savoring the last few days, which I viewed as precious jewels of time. I had formed many friendships and undergone the most transformative experience of my entire life. I now had a new tool belt with which to face the challenges of life, a shift of awareness to my inner self. Some events are indescribable; only a feeling remains that something fundamental has changed and we will never be the same again. I will be forever grateful for this place of love, light, and healing, and the dawn of a happier future. It was without a doubt the most empowering experience I had ever had, as if I'd returned home from a long journey.

Realizations in the Jungle

Those individuals who have traveled the path of yoga to self-realization have said that the vehicle of truth and awareness is not an easy ride. And that you must face yourself, and bring awareness to your ego and mind-constructed delusions over and over in order to discover your divine nature. Bringing awareness to your thought processes invokes the witnessing presence, and as you do this, you're able to realize that you are not your thoughts. This is often referred to as meditation.

Through detached observation of our mind (ego), present moment awareness, and self-study, we can learn new ways to cope with our often painful existence. We suffer for reasons known and unknown, but the ancient teachings of many traditions provide a scientific formula to pull us out of depression, stress, and ignorance and into a reality where we can live an authentically happy, peaceful life. In the pursuit of happiness, the yogic perspective teaches that all beings are a source of the divine. This sets forth compassion and respect for each and every living entity, and shows us that through service to others and cultivating our goodness, we can live a joyous life and fulfill our unique, individual destinies.

L'Eggo My Ego

After my teacher training course, I went straight into offering others what I had learned about the discipline of yoga. I was teaching small groups and private sessions, and I started to notice that some of my students could get into postures that I couldn't. Of course, this was an attack on my sensitive ego, and I began to force myself into advanced postures that my body wasn't ready for and couldn't comfortably accommodate. I used all of my yogic training to dissolve these feelings of comparison, but I didn't have the awareness yet to see my competitiveness for what it was: an ego-instigated episode that would set me up for a painful, self-induced lesson.

One day while I was practicing yoga at home, I decided to see if I could finally get into the hardest of postures for most Westerners, especially men: the Lotus pose. This is where you sit in a cross-legged position and put your feet on opposite thighs. With hips overdeveloped and tight from surfing in cold water, I should have known better, but my ego kept saying, "As a teacher you must be able to achieve this pose." So after a long warmup, I sat on the floor and proceeded to force one ankle over the other on my lap. And I did it! The first time was like the feeling you have when you're on a roller coaster, the weightless plummet and rush of adrenaline as you fall from the apex. I sat there for a few moments and said to myself, "That wasn't as difficult as I thought it would be." So I decided to meditate, since, after all, this was traditionally a meditative posture. I closed my eyes and quieted my mind and tried to ignore the pain building in my knees, thinking that it would subside. After a few minutes, the pain was searing, like my knees were being dipped in boiling water, so I opened my eyes and quickly unwound my legs. As I took both feet simultaneously off of my thighs, I heard a hollow popping sound from both knees. I rolled over onto the ground, gripping my legs in horror, and knew immediately that I had pushed my stiff body too far and done some serious damage to the knees' fragile ligaments.

That was the beginning of a long battle with chronic knee pain and inflammation, and I had to recreate my yoga practice and stop surfing for six months. I was told after an external examination that it was most likely a tear of the MCL and might eventually heal on its own. Naturally optimistic in the face of adversity, I realized that I could still practice many forms and aspects of yoga, and this led me to discover arm-balancing postures and a greater ability to do inversions, which put no pressure on the knees and even aided them in the healing process. I could also still meditate and study spiritual philosophies and teachings; I wouldn't be defeated by the accident.

Through my yogic studies, I also learned the valuable truth that the yoga asana practice is a vehicle to cleanse the body and open the energy channels (nadis) so that you can receive divine awareness, intelligence, and wisdom. Yoga asana is traditionally a preparation for meditation. There is absolutely no reason why anyone should push themselves too hard in their asana practice, no matter what their level. The benefits of yoga asana come through relaxed awareness and concentration on the breath or a focal point (drishti), not through twisting or contorting your body into different positions in order to compete with others. It was a tough lesson to learn, but after I realized the error of listening to and acting from my ego, my yoga practice became a lot more enjoyable and light-hearted.

We are taught in American society to see our life events as good or bad, when in fact, the perceived worst situations can actually turn out to be great opportunities for growth and change. This may be one of the biggest challenges that we face: to not judge what happens to us as a curse or a blessing, and to accept our experiences with faith that everything happens for a reason. I now understood that this incident was another stepping stone to greater clarity and wisdom; by recognizing that my ego was the driving force behind the injury, I became more aware of my ego, and that is the first step to transcending it and observing it from a detached perspective. This was the lesson I learned, but as in my past, I learned it the hard way; and as my awareness grew, I'd be tested again in another aspect of my life. I was to encounter an ethical test as I made my way through the first steps of the Eightfold path of yoga.

Ethical Misconduct in the Realm of Saints

It was the first time I had assisted with a yoga teacher training, and I was honored by and grateful for the opportunity to be of service to the teachers I had studied under. I was nervous about being onstage in front of fifty-plus students, but this was my opportunity to overcome that fear. I knew that I would be in a positive, safe environment because it was the same training that I had taken in the tropics two years earlier; and what better place to practice my skills as a teacher? But being a teacher meant that students would see me in a different light; I was no longer a fellow student but a person who was supposed to be living according to the ethical guidelines set forth by those who came before me. With my animal sexual instincts driving my mind and body, I would fall into the well of desire and passion and learn a lesson of the student/teacher relationship.

I first saw her on the main dirt road of the quiet beach town, a few days before the training began. Her long, blonde hair blew in the wind as she passed me on her red cruiser bicycle, her little black dog riding in the basket attached to the handlebars. I had an intuition that I knew her, but as many beautiful women have ridden across the window of my life, I didn't think much about it as she disappeared around a corner. To my delight, I saw her again at the restaurant where I stopped to eat, and I was again mesmerized by her beauty and grace. Because I was shy, and since she didn't seem to notice me, I watched her walk by, hoping that I'd eventually get to meet her if she was staying in the area.

At the beginning of the training program there she was, one of the students in the course, walking up the stairs toward me with a big smile. I welcomed her to the center and introduced myself, and we had a short chat, our eyes meeting warmly. I was aware of the ethical code of yoga teachers, and tried to suppress the attraction with right thought and speech. This meant that I wouldn't view her as a sexual object or speak to her in a flirtatious manner. But I wasn't into set rules and laws for each and every situation, and the code of conduct was still a question mark in my mind. I had yet to learn the consequences of violating the rules of the teacher/student relationship. Yoga's moral and ethical codes of conduct are there for a reason, set forth and passed down through the ages by sages and seers who have trodden the same route.

As the course progressed, I transcended my fear of speaking in front of a large audience, a development that was deeply transformative and affected me on many levels. The students were enjoying my classes and workshops, and I found my poise as a teacher. I had also started a friendship with the woman I was infatuated with, and we would meet at the beach for sunsets and take walks as the tide caressed our ankles. I was single and in search of a partner, and I fell for her quickly. Before I knew it I was blindly falling in love. The heart-opening curriculum of the program amplified my already intense feelings. We became intimate and kept our relationship separate from the program, but she started to pull away as I became closer. This led me to think about her even more, even though she had stated in our first conversation that she was taking a break from relationships. I had heard her loud and clear, but hoped that she would feel different with time and after the course was over.

In the middle of the month-long training, one of my close friends died in an airplane accident in which he was the pilot. I had been a passenger a few times, with him at the helm of the same plane in which he had the fatal accident; and we had had close calls and terrifying experiences on several of those occasions. Once, we were going over a mountain range, and the fuel pump stalled for five horrifying seconds as the engine shut off and we freefell into the clouds below. Another time, the plane's tachometer stopped working at the same time that a beeping sound came on, and the instrument panel showed that a cylinder was malfunctioning. We were over the ocean and hours away from the coast, and even though he assured me that everything was OK, I prayed that we would make it to our destination safely. Each time, he'd navigated us back to safety. He loved to fly and was an experienced pilot with a well-equipped plane, and he died doing what he loved to do.

My teachers empathized and told me that I didn't have to finish the training, that I could take some time to mourn. I decided to take a few days off to grieve for my deceased friend, and I drove aimlessly for hours from the beach into the thick jungle terrain of Central America. I didn't have a destination in mind; maybe I'd unexpectedly find a unique place in which to contemplate and meditate in nature. As I was driving up a steep mountain in the middle of nowhere, my car suddenly started sputtering, and then the engine turned off with a hiccup. I had enough momentum to pull over to the side of the barren road, and I knew that the problem had most likely occurred because I had taken the car to a mechanic the week before to check out the battery and he'd advised me to replace it. After several unsuccessful attempts to restart it, I surrendered and went to look for a phone or a ride, although I hadn't seen a house or business in miles.

I trudged up the hill in the searing tropical heat, hoping that I would get a better view from the top to see if there was anything within sight. Sweating abundantly and feeling faint, I arrived at the top of the hill, overlooking a beautiful vista; however, it was all lush, green jungle, and if there was a building of some sort, it was swallowed by the rainforest. I walked a little bit farther up the road, and that's when I saw what looked like a house deep in the canopy. I cautiously approached on the narrow but well-trodden path, and came upon an old man with his eyes closed, silently swaying back and forth in a leather rocking chair. "Perdón, Señor," I said, interrupting his slumber. He slowly opened one eye and looked at me like he was dreaming this tall, lanky white man standing in front of him, so I repeated myself to be polite.

"Hola, amigo," he welcomed me, coming to his senses. I explained my dilemma in simple terms and asked if he had a car or a phone, hoping to call a friend or get a ride to the nearest gas station. He laughed heartily, showing his decaying teeth, and I was unsure if he had understood me. Then he put out his hands in a bowl-shaped gesture, apparently wanting some money for the use of his phone or services. I gladly gave him a few dollars, which he shoved into his tattered overalls, and with a smile he pointed beyond his house to another small building that I hadn't seen.

As I walked toward the shanty, a pack of ravenous-looking dogs appeared out of the foliage and surrounded me, barking and wailing. I stood still in fright as the smallest dog broke from the circle and nipped at my heels. I could see the old man, still rocking in his chair and oblivious to my plight, but I didn't want to infuriate the dogs more by crying out for help. Out of the shanty a woman emerged, wielding a broom. In a strong voice she yelled at the dogs, and they immediately dispersed. I graciously thanked her, putting my hands together in a universal symbol of respect and gratitude, and she invited me into her abode, where I explained my situation as best I could in her language. She listened intently and then, with a raised finger and a smile, walked into another room. To my disbelief, she returned carrying a battery charger! I couldn't believe it and was overjoyed; luck had struck in an unbelievable way. This meant that I would have to walk in the blistering sun down the hill into the valley below, retrieve my car's battery, and then carry it back up to charge it. After a glass of the woman's homemade hibiscus cooler, I walked re-energized past the old man and the now sleeping pack of dogs into the valley below.

As I walked down the hill, I pondered how fortunate I was to have found the house, and friendly inhabitants with a battery charger in such a remote location. Having calmly surrendered to my predicament, I did the only thing I could do, which was to go look for help; and by accepting the situation, I found the help I was looking for. Once I arrived at the car, I took out the greasy battery, wrapped it in a towel, and began the trek back up the steep hill.

When I was halfway to the summit, a dark formation of rain clouds began a rapid approach from behind a mountain in the south. Within minutes a torrential downpour ensued, a common occurrence during the rain season. The rain drenched me and made the climb slippery and more treacherous. I wondered if this was my karma for breaking the ethical conduct of the student/teacher relationship, but I laughed in spite of the challenging situation, and the rain actually felt good and cleansed my sweaty body.

I finally made it back to the house. A rumor had already spread that a gringo needed help, and now there were a dozen locals eagerly waiting for me. They laughed as I approached, soaking wet and hauling the battery in my long arms. They sat around me as I connected the battery to the charger, setting off sparks and crackles to add to the excitement. After the battery had been charging for a few minutes, we heard a popping sound and the power went out. One of the men seemed to know what it was and opened a cabinet, revealing the faulty wiring. He turned an electric breaker off and on, and with screams of delight from the crowd, the power came back on. After about an hour of pleasant conversation, I figured that my battery was charged enough, and I gave them what money I had in gratitude and thanked them for their hospitality.

Ethical Misconduct in the Realm of Saints

It was clear skies again, and two of the younger boys accompanied me back to my car and helped to install the recharged battery. I was relieved when it started on the first attempt, and with a long wave goodbye, I took off in hopes of making it back to my lodging before dark without the car breaking down again. As the orange sun set over the shadowy horizon, I thought about my friend who had died in the plane crash, the magical yoga training with which I was assisting, and the woman I had fallen in love with. From a yogic perspective, I was learning to refrain from viewing things as good or bad, regardless of my judgment or opinion about the situation; but my mind was filled with contrasting emotions of sadness, joy, and heartfelt pain, extinguishing these principles.

Upon my return, I was happy to find on my doorstep a poetic letter from my intimate friend. She expressed her tender feelings for me, but she also explained that she needed her space to absorb what she was learning in the program. I didn't want to ruin her experience, so I backed off; we remained close friends throughout the rest of the course and ended up spending our last few days together at a hot-spring resort in a romantic setting before she flew home. This was torture for me, because we lived on opposite coasts and I had a strong feeling that we'd probably never see each other again, knowing that she didn't want a relationship. Unrequited love may be one of the most painful emotional challenges, and there's nothing you can do to change things if the chemistry isn't present for both people.

All things considered, I had gone against the ethical guidelines of yoga by breaking the rules of teacher/student conduct, even though I'd been led by my heart. Many months after the program, when my feelings for her had subsided, I looked back and realized that I'd sabotaged my own experience more than anything. I was undoubtedly still learning how to avoid suffering by heeding the advice of those before me.

The path to happiness involves continually refining awareness and making proper choices. Sometimes even our best intentions are met with disastrous results, but we can choose at any time to find meaning in the experience, learn a lesson, and move on with a positive disposition. For whatever reason, I've had to learn the same lessons many times before finally waking up to the meaning. But when I accept myself as I am, the chains of regret and self-loathing dissolve, and I walk on with knowledge of what has caused me suffering and how to keep from reliving the same mistake. However, as long as we're here, new lessons will arise, and it wasn't long before I stepped into the yoga arena again and created "quite a wonderful mess," as one of my esteemed spiritual teachers put it.

Reef Cuts and Bali Bombing

Eight of us boarded a boat for a two-week journey through the Indian Ocean in search of uncrowded, flawless waves. We had planned the journey almost a year in advance, so all of us were excited when we met our captain at the boat harbor after the long flight from California to Jakarta, Indonesia. Along with the boat's captain, there were a few deck hands and a chef, and we were all ready to take off on our mission to uncharted surf spots halfway across the world. I had butterflies in my stomach as we drifted out into the open ocean, but I knew that this would be an exciting quest.

Our sleeping arrangement was scattered bunk beds in the hull of the boat. My bed happened to be right under the frosty AC unit and too short for my lanky, six-foot-three frame. I had never been on a boat trip into the deep sea except for a one-day fishing excursion, and I'd vomited overboard many times on that outing as I tried to find my sea legs. Remembering this, I lay down in my bunk at the onset of the voyage, and did breathing exercises to calm myself as the boat rocked back and forth to the rise and fall of the ocean. I felt nauseous but eager to surf the waves I had seen many times in magazines and videos, and I hoped the knot in my stomach would subside in time.

After a full day's travel, we anchored in a pristine bay with point breaks on both sides of us. Like children entering an amusement park, we screamed with delight and jumped off the side of the boat one by one into the warm, crystal-clear ocean. We surfed nonstop, only taking breaks to eat delicious food prepared by our private chef. This trip was turning out to be a wonderful experience, and we also had some herbal goodies to make us feel at home. These herbal remedies had aided in calming my stomach, and I had only vomited overboard once, in the beginning after we left port.

The next day the waves were dreamlike at a left point fabled for its long rides. Often, at other times during our trip, the captain informed us that other boats would be pulling into the bay carrying eight to twelve hungry surfers; but today it was just our crew, and we were taking advantage of the situation. All of us took turns riding waves and hooting to each other on the paddle back out for our next ride—all of us, that is, except one wave-hungry friend on a longboard. He would frantically paddle around everyone and take off on whatever wave he chose, regardless of whose turn it was. After his wave-hog attitude became too much to bear, some of us started to yell obscenities and drop in on him.

I had had enough. After everyone else went in for lunch, I was patiently waiting way up on the point for my last wave. I could see the wave hog's bald head bobbing up and down as he paddled full-speed from the inside after getting a wave, to go around me to take position for the oncoming set. I knew that I was already about as far out as you could be and still make the section of the wave that would open up into the bay, so I just let him go by. I said to myself, "If he takes off inside of me, I'm going to drop in on him." This, of course, was my ego speaking, and there was an immediate karmic consequence to the premeditated decision to take off on him, possibly causing him injury if he fell onto the razor-sharp reef.

Sure enough, he cut inside of me as I was paddling to get the best wave of the set, and I screamed that I was going on it and to back off. He chose not to listen and somehow managed to get to his feet in the most critical part of the wave, but since it was twenty yards inside of me, I had more than enough time to take off in front of him. As I was bottom turning, I could see him desperately trying to make it around the section, but I was in the perfect position, and since I had been waiting patiently for the wave, I felt justified in continuing in front of him. I turned in harmony with the wave, and I could see my spray hitting him in the face as I maneuvered off the top. Finally, he got too far behind and fell in the whitewater, while I made the section and continued the long ride toward the boat waiting in the channel. The boys were watching from the railing, pumping their fists as I finished the wave and he was washed into the shallow impact zone.

"Oh man, you roasted him!" one friend peppered with glee as I boarded the boat.

"It's his fault," I responded vindictively, "that's what happens when you paddle around people and don't wait your turn." Everyone knew the unwritten law of surfing: Don't be greedy and try to take every wave. This was a golden rule and he had broken it, which at the time I felt justified my actions.

He finally made it back to the boat; I could tell he was very unhappy as he climbed the ladder with a vicious scowl and a beet-red face. He immediately started cussing at me, and I calmly stated my case: He had taken that wave out of turn and I had been waiting for it. His face looked like something out of a horror movie. Spit flew from his mouth as he tried to belittle me in front of everyone. The boat looked like a gladiator pit, he and I on each end and the crew gathered around us in a circle, waiting to see what would happen. After I had heard enough, my ego spoke for me again and told him to do something about it. He took a step forward, stopped and looked at me with bitter contempt, then retreated from the scene with a few more inflammatory comments.

This made the journey uncomfortable for him and me, and we didn't speak to each other for a few days, until I finally decided to break the ice. He defended his position, and I felt like I had to apologize, as I didn't want to have bad vibes for the rest of the boat trip. He accepted and we shook hands, and we actually ended up becoming better friends because of the incident. However, the karmic debt was still to be paid; ultimately, the situation between us had been my fault. I had the awareness in retrospect to see that I could have just let him take that wave and waited for the next, thus avoiding the conflict. This would have been the true path of nonviolence toward others, but sometimes we don't observe right action in the heat of the moment, when we're being ruled by our ego and emotions.

We arrived at another famous left point break a few days later, but this time there were four boats in front of the break and about thirty surfers in the water. I waited until a few people went in, as a respectful gesture to the crowd, and then took my position in the line upon the shoulder. Finally, after a long set during which everyone else took a wave, my turn came. But one guy who had just got a wave paddle-battled me deeper into the takeoff zone and made it around me to take position. I wasn't going to drop in on him in uncharted waters, so I let him go, but to my surprise he backed off and shouted for me to go. I only had a split second to turn around and stroke into it, but as I stood up, I could see that I was hopelessly deep and was going to get pitched over the falls. I could hear him laughing as the wave sucked off of the reef underneath me and I was thrown feet-first into the sharp coral heads. It felt like someone was hitting me all over with a hammer as I hit the reef again and again, trying to protect my face with my hands, screaming underwater for the beating to stop. I was unmercifully washed a hundred yards to the inside, and I stood up in knee-deep water to retrieve my board. I was hurt, how badly I didn't know, but my back felt ripped apart and I had a multitude of deep cuts and abrasions all over my body. I gingerly got on my board and paddled back to the boat in pain.

Once aboard, I took off my wetsuit jacket. A friend squeezed lime over the cuts, and the man I'd had a confrontation with kindly picked the pieces of reef out of my hip. I had lacerated my entire back and taken chunks of flesh out of many parts of my body, but thankfully, my wetsuit jacket and reef booties had prevented me from being more seriously injured. I lay in my cramped bunk bed for a day and a half and tried to sleep off the pain, using only tea tree oil on the cuts because it was all that I had brought in my first-aid kit. Others were sliced and diced from the reef as well, and they hoarded their healing salves, which was understandable, since we were far from home and had another week on the boat.

Eventually, the cuts on my back turned lime green from being constantly damp and unable to heal in the humid environment, but I knew that going home wasn't an option. We were a day away from any port, and unless you called in a rescue helicopter or got a ride from another boat heading to shore, you were stuck on the boat you came in on. So even though I was in physical pain, with multiple scratches across my back and past injuries flaring up, I tried to block it out and surf as much as I could for the rest of the journey.

The positive side of the voyage was that we traveled through the nights with the stars guiding our way, to end up at a new surf spot every morning, often without another boat in sight. Sometimes, through the foggy morning mist we'd see a boat in the distance, and we'd pull anchor and head out to a new, private destination. Our captain was a master of sea navigation and knew the area, so we always found fun waves. The food prepared by our comical Australian chef was at first eyes-in-the-back-of-the-head delicious, but toward the end, when our food supplies were down to white rice and multicolored cookies, I daydreamed of a freshly cooked meal and a piece of homemade boysenberry pie.

We were all ready to get off of the boat at the end of our trip, so when we disembarked it was with a mixture of gratitude and relief. After housing eight men for two weeks, the sleeping quarters had turned into a musty, foul-smelling dungeon. We took another boat to the island of Bali to surf, check out the sights, and heal our wounds. Bali is a magical place, and we had planned to stay there for a week or two, but after a few days of partying, I had a strong desire to go home, as I was feeling sick from the reef cuts and needed some personal space. The rest of the group were also going their separate ways, so I made arrangements to fly back to California a week early. I knew that I needed to see a doctor right away, as the reef cuts on my back were turning a darker shade of green and I was starting to get a low-grade fever.

I barely made it to a hotel upon my return to the States, and I got sick as soon as I entered my room. I fell into a nightmarish sleep with violent dreams and slept for two days, only getting up to use the bathroom and drink some water. I'd left the television on, and I awoke one night to a news bulletin being broadcast from the island of Bali. "Is this a dream?" I thought in my feverish delirium. To my stomach-clenching horror, the newscaster stated that a terrorist bombing had occurred on Bali, at the two infamous clubs where we had partied just before leaving the island. Hundreds of people were dead or injured, and the nightclubs had been literally erased from the earth in the blast. I started freaking out when I realized that had we not left the island a week early, our group most likely would have been partying at these clubs and possibly injured or dead!

Another near-death accident had rocked my world, and I felt blessed and grateful to have had the intuition to leave early, even if that intuition was born from the reef cuts on my back. Now I was thankful for the surfing accident; maybe I would have stayed longer had I been injury-free. The mystery of my life, of why I had been spared so many times, was on my mind as I fell into another two days of nightmares and fitful sleep.

As I recovered, I had a lot of time to think about the meaning of life. I decided I must have some type of purpose or potential yet to be fulfilled. Why else would I still be alive after so many accidents and near-death experiences? I'd had many realizations about my true nature, but my purpose and potential remained a mystery. I knew that I just needed to stay on my spiritual path and do the best I could. In time the truth would be revealed, and I would discover the gift for humanity that I had inside of me—the gift that we all have but is often hidden under layers of social conditioning and cultural brainwashing. I would come to learn that this universal gift is simple: to love yourself and others, and to contribute to the world in a positive way for the benefit of future generations.

Zorba the Buddha

It has been said that a guru, or "awakened one," comes into your life when you're ready, if spiritual guidance is what you seek. As a teenager, I skateboarded by a building that was said to be a sex-cult center directed by a deranged guru from India. All of the participants wore orange clothing, and all over town I'd see the orange people who labeled themselves the "Rajneesh." Sometimes, out of curiosity, I'd sit on a bench outside of their gatherings and listen to the cries and screams of joy and ecstasy; but, ignorant and afraid of the unknown, I would just laugh at how crazy they were. Little did I know then that these people were following a spiritual teacher who would change my life many years in the future.

He went by many names, but the most well-known is Osho. When I was seeking guidance later in my life, this enlightened man's teachings would affect me in profound ways and further aid me on my path of self-discovery. As a guru to millions of lost souls across the planet, he offered those who cared to listen a path to true happiness. His unorthodox and controversial teachings led him in the

1970s from his birthplace of India to the United States, where a multitude of Westerners were attracted to the light he shined as an awakened being. He was said to have been poisoned by his enemies and to have nearly died when put in jail for the crimes of a few of his fanatical followers, and there were rumors that he was considered a very dangerous man by the U.S. government. After being deported back to India, he recovered and lived out his days guiding others and building his dream center which, decades after his death, is still a destination for countless people from every country and walk of life.

When I discovered his teachings, I was deep into my spiritual studies, and I related to his confrontational practice of questioning religious dogma, all spiritual philosophies, and social and political establishments. His discourses on numerous subjects, and his translations of ancient sutras and scriptures, brought me to a new level of awareness that shattered the paradigm I'd been living under. The more I learned and absorbed of his life's work, the more I was humbled and understood the path to self-realization.

Zorba the Buddha

One of the more interesting aspects of this man was that he wanted to create the conditions for a new human being called Zorba the Buddha, who would enjoy earthly existence while living the serenity of a Buddha, or awakened being. Osho developed scientific methods and techniques for this awakening, with meditation as the foundation of his approach. Osho had unconditional love for every living being, and like other saints, Buddhas, and religious figures, he was on earth for a short time, misunderstood and persecuted by some and revered by millions. His sphere of influence reached me at a critical point in my life, when I was questioning my path and looking for a new route to freedom and joy. He showed me that the only real route is the inner journey, during which questions cease and the truth is revealed: We are what we seek.

Dream Manifested

Several years after my initial yoga training, I had an opportunity to fulfill a long-term dream of mine: to open a yoga studio in my hometown. I had a close friend who was a dedicated yogi; he had experience running a studio and wanted to be my co-director. The dream became a reality when, after multiple conversations with the leasing agent, he contacted me to sign a two-year agreement. I remembered that one of my teachers, who ran her own yoga studio, had suggested that I just teach yoga and avoid opening a studio because of the business hardships involved. But I went against her advice and signed the contract anyway, thinking that it would be a huge success and a way for me to offer my knowledge about the path of yoga to the community I'd grown up in.

I had no idea what I was getting myself into. The space needed a lot of work before I could open the doors to the public. I stopped my recreational cannabis usage so that I would have clarity and focus for the job at hand, and I felt free, dedicated to opening a yoga studio where people could practice this path of freedom and joy. My life had changed dramatically since I had adopted the teachings of sages and seers, lessons left by enlightened beings to guide mankind toward self-realization. This would be a chance for me to share with others what I had learned.

The seemingly never-ending remodel ended up costing twice as much as planned, and I was trying to hire yoga teachers at the same time. This was a task in itself, as not many teachers wanted to work more than two shifts a week in a town saturated with yoga, or else they were already committed to another studio. I ended up hiring fifteen teachers to fill the six-classes-a-day schedule, and this is when the chaos and calamities began.

After I signed the binding lease agreement, my friend who'd wanted to be co-director informed me that he wasn't going to be able to do so; he was going to India to be a vagabond after breaking up with his long-term girlfriend. I'd been counting on his experience running a yoga studio, but, proud and ignorant, I thought I could do it alone, without any experience or help. I was trying to remain centered throughout the process, but the universe was testing my patience and maturity by overwhelming me with dozens of tasks and projects, and the grand opening was getting pushed farther and farther into the future.

After two long months, during which I used up my entire savings for the project, we were ready to open, and I had attracted great local teachers who were excited about the new yoga space. The mall where the studio was located was outdated, and many of the other spaces were unoccupied, but we would have the only yoga studio on this side of town, and the buzz had started from word of mouth and advertising in local publications. Everything seemed like it was coming together perfectly until the first teacher meeting, when all of us got together at the studio for our first forum.

The fifteen teachers arrived on time. Some had years of experience and a local following, while others were new to teaching yoga but enthusiastic about the opportunity. They sat around me in a half circle, and after a few minutes of silence, I read a passage from a book by the son of an infamous yogi. The passage dealt with what it is to be a yoga teacher, and it bonded us in our collective intention to be of service to others. I then proceeded to break down the workings of the studio and payment guidelines.

Dream Manifested

One outspoken teacher, with whom I had previously had a challenging encounter, starting talking over me and the others. She had arrived late to her initial interview, and when the next interviewee arrived, she didn't have the courtesy to leave; instead, she extended her time by inviting the next candidate to join us and then talking over her when she answered my questions. Now, true to her nature, every time I opened my mouth she cut me off with a sarcastic comment and then stared at me as if to say, "Where is your breaking point?" I tried to remain calm and centered in my new role as studio director, but she was testing my patience, and her obnoxious demeanor was putting other teachers on edge as well. I was a neophyte in these waters of unconditional compassion for others, and I had only a little knowledge of how to run a yoga studio, but I remained focused and listened intently to everyone's comments and suggestions. The argumentative teacher began to bicker with other teachers as they stated their viewpoints, which is when I snapped. I told her to please be quiet and let other people speak. She glared at me with fury and immediately began packing her bag to leave.

Dream Manifested

I suggested that we take a short break, at which point the meeting became chaotic, and the teachers talked among themselves about studio issues. When I returned from the bathroom, all of the teachers were leaving, and I was unable to finish what I had to say or gather everyone together to chant the customary "Om." I was devastated. I felt like a failure as a director, but all I could do was to wish them a good evening and adjourn the meeting.

I had a profound realization in the quiet studio after everyone had left: Most modern-day yoga teachers were just like anyone else, and teaching yoga didn't mean that you were a perfect person. Most were ordinary people going through the ups and downs of life, and many taught yoga simply as a means to make an extra income. With yoga often misperceived as a form of exercise in the West, and teaching certificates given after weekend trainings, how could an individual possibly learn and authentically teach this 5,000-year-old discipline? I personally felt that I was more of a student than a yoga authority, but I knew that I could only teach from my own experience and try to help guide people back to their own hearts as I guided myself to mine.

After we opened the doors to the public, slowly but surely people started taking classes, especially from the teachers with a local following. The popular teachers numbered about five of the fifteen, but we did have over one hundred new students in the first month. My own classes had a decent turnout of friends, teachers, and newcomers. I was happy with the way the business was going and starting to feel comfortable in my new role as a director.

By nature I was a reclusive person, and within a few weeks of opening, I found myself dealing with business, people, and questions all day, which left me physically and mentally exhausted. One fateful day, when I was extremely tired and overwhelmed, I sold a monthly pass to a couple that had been consistently taking classes at the studio. After they left, I locked the doors and decided to go home to rest. While I was driving, my cell phone started ringing, hidden somewhere among the scattered piles of paperwork all over my passenger seat. I was approaching the scene of a non-injury accident, with a Highway Patrol vehicle and two officers attending, and I slowed down with the line of cars at the stoplight. The light turned green, and my cell phone rang again as the cars in front of me regained their traveling speed. I accelerated and reached for my phone, and when I looked up there was a big white truck at a dead stop in front of me. I was now going thirty miles per hour and had only a millisecond to react, and I slammed into the back of the truck without braking.

The sound of breaking glass and metal impacting metal filled the air. I looked over to see the two dumbfounded officers ten feet away shaking their heads—I had crashed into another vehicle right next to the previous accident. They could see that I was wearing my seatbelt and unharmed, so they waved for me to pull over, and I backed up and drove around to the driver's side of the truck I had hit to see if the passengers were all right.

To my alarm, they were slumped into each other and moaning in pain. My heart racing, I asked if they were OK. The driver tentatively raised his head and looked at me in bewilderment. To my surprise, it was the couple who had just bought a monthly yoga pass! I had unintentionally chased them down and smashed into them from behind after they had left the studio, and I was beyond embarrassment. The man politely smiled and told his partner, "Honey, get up. It's the yoga studio director." She raised her head to greet me.

"I'm so sorry. Are you guys hurt?" I asked nervously.

"Oh, we're fine, just uh, you know, a little shaken up," the driver responded kindly.

The officers walked over to our cars and saw that we were fine and that it was just a minor fender bender. They informed us that another patrol car would be coming to take the report because they had been there for hours with the other accident. After they left, we surveyed our cars and decided to shake hands and deal with the damage separately, which was a big relief for me, since I had caused the accident. "What a way to end a day," I thought as I drove home, my bumper making an annoying scraping sound against my front tire.

The first few months after opening, the studio seemed to be doing well for a new business, but we were still deep in the red, and I desperately needed some help with the accounting and management. That's when disaster struck. A thirty-day rain resulted in a gigantic landslide on my property, and a piece of my house drifted away like a chunk of ice breaking off of a glacier. This was a huge financial setback that happened to coincide with identity theft by an online fraud. To add to my challenges, teachers were calling me all day, canceling or needing subs for their classes, and I was running the business by myself while trying to refinance my house and take care of the identity infiltration. Things were going downhill fast, and I fell back into my old pattern of using pot to numb myself to my life. At first, it seemed to work. It soothed my tired mind and afforded me deep, dreamless sleep, but the medicinal herb also has negative effects when used excessively; I was unable to deal with employees and clientele because I was so high, and it enhanced my reclusive nature.

I decided to take a much-needed few days off and go to my secret retreat, to meditate and get away from it all so that I could consider my options. During that time, I had an epiphany: I was going to lose either my house or the studio due to my financial crisis, and I had to choose which one was more important. With sadness, I knew that I was going to lose the yoga studio; I needed a place to live, and I had a lot more invested in my house.

The dreaded day came when I typed up an e-mail to all of the teachers, informing them that the studio would be closing after only a few short months. This ignited a variety of responses, from gratitude to anger; one teacher berated me with words that pierced my heart and led to an e-mail war. In her e-mail, she attacked me, accusing me of causing financial hardship for all of the teachers, as many of them had quit teaching at other studios to work at mine. She had sent her initial reply as a group e-mail for all of the teachers to read, and I responded to the group, trying to explain myself and the tight spot I was in. She ended up apologizing to me, and we ended our war of words amicably. I realized that it was my fault; I had chosen to open the studio without experience or preparation for such an undertaking. But ultimately, the demise of the studio resulted from unforeseen financial setbacks, and I had given it my best.

After all the natural disasters and studio dramas, I felt humbled, but I also felt that I had been successful in some ways, even though the business had reached a disastrous end. I had taken a risk and explored my passions; this in itself was an accomplishment to me. Life often throws curveballs at us when we least expect it, but with a shift of perspective and an acceptance of fate, we can get back up after a hard fall and see the bright side of every situation. Even after the shattering of my dream of opening a yoga studio, I knew that I had to practice non-attachment to the outcome or else cause myself unnecessary suffering by regretting the events that had led to the studio's downfall. I would continue traveling down the river of self-realization. Where it would lead I wasn't sure, but I was committed to the journey and ready to follow my heart into a new chapter of my life with more wisdom and maturity.

The Pancha Karma Experience

Now in my mid-thirties and having traveled a multi-dimensional life path, I discovered a healing modality that would bring me greater health and clarity. I had overcome many health issues, stemming from a congenital underdeveloped immune system and an unbalanced diet in my formative years, by dedicating myself to a wholesome diet and studying nutrition from both Eastern and Western perspectives as an adult. And I would move on to experience one of the oldest health traditions, which has been well documented and beneficial to humanity since time immemorial: Ayurveda.

Ayurveda (science of life) and its complementary therapy, Pancha Karma, employed for the health and integration of mind, body, and spirit, are, compared to yoga, relatively new to the West. India is the birthplace of Ayurveda, which was initially intended to help royal families sustain their youth so that they could rule longer, with continued health and vitality. This age-old medical science is now becoming one of the latest alternative therapies to make its mark in the West, used to treat a myriad of ailments and illnesses and also as a time-tested way to detoxify and revitalize your entire being.

I was initiated into the healing science of Ayurveda at a beautiful private retreat called Tierra de Los Mangos. As a holistic health counselor and yoga enthusiast, I was interested in Ayurveda, aware that it is the mother of these disciplines. I was having problems with high levels of mercury in my system and had been trying to rid my body and tissues of this poisonous toxic metal for a few years. After trying all types of alternative therapies with no results, I was referred to an Ayurvedic practitioner who informed me of his system's gentle approach to removing the mercury.

After my initial consultation, I decided to journey to the retreat in Central America, where I would spend a week doing the royal Ayurvedic treatments of Pancha Karma. I was advised that although the therapies could be revitalizing, there were usually side effects from the toxins released from the body and, typically, some emotional distress. Since I had been living a health-conscious lifestyle for many years, including a daily yoga and meditation practice, I figured that I would be on the low end of the spectrum for undesirable side effects and emotional imbalance.

The preparation for the treatments started a week before my trip, with the transition to a light diet: preferably only kitcheri (mung bean soup) and a substance called "tikta ghee," increasing the dosage by a tablespoon each day until I arrived at the retreat. Ghee is clarified butter; tikta ghee is an herbal-infused ghee that starts the process of stripping your intestinal tract of the toxic plaque that accumulates from years of undigested matter and buildup. The first cup of ginger tea mixed with a tablespoon of tikta ghee was bearable but hard to swallow. It left me with a heavy feeling and coated my tongue with a fatty film, but chased with a lime, it wasn't that bad! However, by the third day, up to a dose of three tablespoons, I could barely swallow the greasy tea. I had to imagine that I was taking a shot of liquor at a bar, with my friends cheering me on and a lime chaser to follow as quickly as possible. After day five of the light diet and home-based preparation therapies, which also included plenty of rest, I figured that the worst was almost over and I was ready for the luxurious Ayurvedic body therapies and relaxing treatments I had heard about.

The Pancha Karma Experience

When I arrived at the retreat, I was assaulted by a dream world of rich colors, sounds, and smells of the jungle. It was an extraordinarily peaceful environment. A waterfall tumbled into a tiled pool with a dolphin mosaic and guardian statues in the center. The rich green of the palms and foliage was in direct contrast to the vibrant sponged papaya color of the Euro-Colombian architecture. I was led to my room by the caretaker and was pleased by the canopy bed and stylish teak furniture. The scenic views of the jungle immediately changed my mood from travel-weary to completely relaxed, and I drifted off into a deep sleep for a midday siesta on my comfortable bed.

I awoke to a soft knock on the door and opened it to find my two Pancha Karma therapists. I had talked to one of them on the phone; she had an attractive voice and we'd had a nice conversation, but I was stunned by their beauty and immediately had mixed feelings about the situation. I was well aware of the possible pitfalls in the teacher/student or therapist/client relationship, in which an emotional connection could take away from or jeopardize the therapy or teachings. Nevertheless, I was still human, and I was not sure if I would be relaxed receiving Abhyanga (the four-handed oil massage) and other intimate

The Pancha Karma Experience

treatments from two attractive women. They introduced themselves and explained that I would be on a soup-based diet and that I had to take one last six-tablespoon serving of the tikta ghee. I was just getting over being sick to my stomach from the last dose, and I cringed. "Really?" Their response was accompanied by a smile. "Yes, you don't look oily enough." They further broke down the protocol over a cup of ginger tea, and I was set at ease by their joyous nature and authentic professionalism.

Day one of the luxurious Pancha Karma therapies was amazing, just what I had hoped for. I was treated to seven therapies, including four-handed massage with specific oils for your constitution (Abhyanga), steam therapy to absorb the oils (Swedana), then an herbal grain body scrub to remove the toxins (Garshana), followed by an eye wash (Netra Tarpanam), sinus cleanse (Nasya), and throat gargle (Kaval), before going back to the table to receive an herbal enema (Basti).

I had managed to relax and meditate through the four-handed massage even though I'd enjoyed it a little too much, so I knew that I had overcome a hurdle and a possibly embarrassing situation. But the humiliation of oiling up and inserting a tube in my anus in front of the therapist wasn't something I had anticipated, and my pelvic floor was now miserably contracted. The therapist relaxed me with light conversation and told me to breathe, releasing any tension on the exhale. Now, insertion complete, I looked up in horror at the gallon of warm liquid that I was to retain for twenty minutes in my colon! As I lay on my side, feeling the oils penetrate tissues deep inside me, there came a point when I needed a break, and I asked her to stop the stream of the fluid. Amazingly, I had taken in all of the herbal liquid, and I was told to switch onto my other side so that the fluid would travel in another direction through my intestinal tract. During the therapy, a light massage of the abdomen was performed to release any obstructions, and when the twenty minutes were up, I signaled that the dam was going to burst so that my therapist could leave and I could release in the adjacent bathroom.

I returned to the table refreshed and thoroughly relaxed for Shirodhara, where a stream of warm, medicated oil is continuously poured onto your forehead for about half an hour. This was said to induce deep relaxation and a meditative state, and after five minutes, although it was pleasurable, I was still coherent. Then, unexpectedly, I fell into a trance in which I saw visions of the past and was greeted by an image of my father, whom I hadn't spoken to in many years. As the cotton was pulled from my eyes to end the session, castor oil-laced tears flooded down my cheeks, and I cried for the first time in many years about my distant relationship with my father.

With day one of the Pancha Karma therapies over, as the brilliant ginger sun descended into the rainforest canopy, I retreated to my room to read and meditate, completely wiped out from the soup-based diet and all of the day's treatments. I wasn't used to feeling so weak and depleted, being an avid surfer with an athletic lifestyle, and I was told to rest and take it easy with lots of sleep, and to drink plenty of herbal tea to keep flushing the internal toxins. I had quit sugar, caffeinated tea, and coffee cold-turkey when I arrived, as well as my recreational cannabis sacrament. As I lay in my bed with my first headache from caffeine withdrawals, I craved my society-sanctioned addictions to take away the pain. I had no appetite, I kept burping up the foul tikta ghee, and my sugar-loving intestinal bacteria screamed for me to feed them. With a building fever and an agitated mind, I slipped into a restless sleep, only to awaken at three a.m., hungry, thirsty, and with a nauseous feeling in my shrunken stomach.

Days three and four were the worst of it; my body, oiled internally and externally, felt loose and relaxed, but I was feeling the debilitating weakness of an eighty-year-old man. The tikta ghee therapy had finally ended, but I was awoken by the therapists and told to drink a purgative concoction that would further eliminate the toxins circulating in my bloodstream and gastrointestinal tract. Nothing could have prepared me for a cup of the most repulsive herbs I'd ever tasted; the horrible, bitter taste froze my throat and made my tongue retreat in shock. My barely awake eyes filled with tears. "Surely this is a poisonous substance and these sorceresses are torturing me for their amusement," I thought in my feverish state. They had these little smiles as I coughed and forcefully swallowed gulps of the horrid brew, but they assured me that in a few hours, I would be having a delicious, purging bowel movement.

I lay in bed in the early morning's tropical heat, drenched in sweat and what seemed like seconds away from vomiting. The therapists, whom I came to think of as the PK angels, cared for me and gave me secret remedies and pills that eased the symptoms. I sucked on a tiny piece of crystal menthol, and in seconds the nausea subsided. The therapists were extensively trained in the healing arts of Pancha Karma and had treated hundreds of clients, and they were well aware of every possible twist and turn of a client's condition. I started to feel better, but the bowel movement never came, and as darkness approached they advised me to drink another cup of the purgative.

"Absolutely not!" I shrieked, like a child forced to eat his vegetables. They knew that I was at my limit, and with compassionate smiles, they agreed that I had had enough for the day.

That night I lay in bed with a clear mind, but my body was still very weak and depleted of its life force. In the privacy of my room I let out an innocent gas bubble, and that's when the anticipated bowel movement happened. For the first time since I was a little baby, I had pooped my pants! The purgative had taken full effect, like a silent ninja in the middle of the night, and a gallon of sludge poured out of my disturbed colon and down my legs. "How disgusting," I whispered as I ran, thighs clenched, to the bathroom. Sounds that usually came only from a stuffed-up vacuum cleaner erupted from within me as I slumped over the toilet in relief. I then took a shower and changed the sheets, and lay back down for some needed sleep. I quickly passed out and awoke to the tranquil sounds of a flowing river. "How nice," I muttered sleepily. It was around three a.m., my new wake-up time, and I went half awake to use the restroom. Shockingly, I put my foot down in a puddle of water that had a blue tinge to it. "Am I hallucinating?" I wondered. I soon found out that my bowel movement had clogged the pipes, and the soft sound that I'd thought was a river was unveiled as the overflowing toilet. I knew enough to turn off the water, and I begrudgingly cleaned up the mess. The gigantic mosquitoes that had gathered over the stinky overflow bit me everywhere, and the nightmare continued as I lay in bed scratching and fighting off the blood-sucking demons as the sun rose.

The last few days of the treatments, I was in a bad mood. I wasn't used to being told what to do, what to eat, and to just rest all day. And to make matters worse, I couldn't go surfing during one of the best swells in years at the world-class surf spots outside the center. But even if I had been cleared to surf, I wouldn't have had the energy. I was cautioned that it takes a lot of energy for the body to go through this healing process, and that it was best to refrain from strenuous activities, including my vigorous yoga asana practice. Also, my bond to one of the PK angels had intensified, and I was starting to fantasize in the oxygen-rich environment. It was a challenging situation that I seemed to be reliving, in different forms, over and over again. Thankfully, from past mistakes I had learned a deference technique to transform the energy that often circulates in such a bonding atmosphere. This practice calmed my misdirected feelings and put me into a mindset of gratefulness and appreciation for the care I was receiving.

Now, after nearly two weeks of preparation and Pancha Karma therapies, I was finished! My mind was clear and focused even though my strength had yet to return. They informed me that the next two weeks would determine how strong I would come back and told me to keep up the soup diet and take it easy. I had lost ten pounds from my slim six-foot-three frame, but I was told that the tissue would return with a newfound strength and vitality.

I made the mistake of sneaking off to go surfing a few days after the treatments ended. I was still feeling weak and depleted, but the waves were perfect and a surfer's heart is always beckoned by the ocean swells. The waves were big, and I got caught inside during a closeout set. My strong paddling arms had been reduced to powerless sticks, and for the first time in many years of surfing, I called out for help as I was thrown into the rocks. Bobbing up and down in an eddy in the reef as eight- to ten-foot waves crashed on my head, I had the dark feeling that death was imminent. But miraculously, the set of waves stopped, and I crawled onto my dinged-up surfboard and was washed onto the beach in the turbulent whitewater. Lying there on the sand, cut and bruised from my thrashing, I thanked heaven that I was alive and relatively unharmed.

I had learned another vital lesson on the path that I had chosen: to pay attention to a therapist's advice and cautions when embarking on such profound healing therapies. On the positive side, the deep cleanse of my body had cleared my mind in a way I couldn't have predicted, and now I was more focused, clearer about my life and purpose: to be of service to others while staying on the path of awareness. Bringing awareness to my thoughts, words, and actions was naturally leading me to my purpose as I connected with the witnessing presence inside of me; that is, pure love and universal intelligence. It has been said that our purpose and potential are revealed only in the present moment, as we disconnect from our ego and its projections into the past and future. The Pancha Karma treatment assisted me in this inner journey, and I would now use the therapies as a valuable tool toward physical and mental well-being and happiness.

The Secret Revealed

I had been practicing visualization techniques for many years, mainly for surfing and in my meditation practice to send others kindness, love, and gratitude. I was extremely inspired after watching *The Secret*, a movie that explains the Law of Attraction in a methodical way. Although the movie is based on material objects and worldly success as external sources of happiness, it also explains a formula that you can practice to bring joy, peace, and love into your life. This natural law, which empowers you to visualize, believe, and manifest your goals and ambitions, added to my interest in the power of visualization, and I was energized to delve deeper into this powerful, life-altering technique.

I decided to do an experiment to see if I could attract my ideal woman through this visualization practice. Following the movie's guidelines, I wrote down exactly what I wanted from a partner, and I drew a picture of how I imagined her on the cover of a writing journal. Every morning, and every night before I went to bed, I would imagine this person in my life and believe that she was searching for me also, and that we would find each other, somehow, when the time was right. I had been single for years after a long list of short-lived relationships, and even though I thought that I was content being alone, my heart yearned for someone to share my life with. I figured that if it was meant to be, then the right woman would enter my life, and applying the Law of Attraction seemed an esoteric and interesting way to summon her.

One morning a few weeks later, sitting on my cushiony couch drinking yerba mate, I had an impulse to browse online personal ads, and I found an ad by a woman who described herself exactly as I had visualized my perfect mate. I had an immediate warm feeling about her in my heart, and I responded and told her my story. She answered that I was the only one she had responded to because she had a good feeling about me, too. After we talked on the phone a few times, we decided to meet in a neighborhood park near her house to get to know each other better.

I knew from the moment I saw her that this was the woman I had visualized and been waiting for my entire life, and when she smiled, I felt a warmth come over me, sending with it a wave of love. She felt the same way, and there was an immediate connection in our first embrace. She was on a similar spiritual path as I, and as we enjoyed our first dinner together, we gazed into each other's eyes and our souls bonded without words. It turned out that she had been using the same technique to attract her ideal mate. We had both used the visualization method to find each other, and the beautiful relationship that formed over time is a testament to the fact that we can manifest things in our lives, consciously or unconsciously, by our thoughts, desires, and intentions.

The Law of Attraction has become an invaluable tool in my life. Even though all dreams may not come to fruition through this principle, it seems that, in time, wishes born of the intention to help others and to develop happiness, love, compassion, and other positive emotions will come to pass in some way or form. And the opposite is true if we're fixated on the ego, which breeds and feeds off of emotional negativity, or external objects, which will never bring us lasting happiness. We undoubtedly create the world that we live in with our thoughts and perceptions of reality. The choice is ours as to what we create and manifest in our lives. By cultivating this natural law, we can attract the things that lead to sustainable happiness, bringing us and others closer to our purpose and infinite potential by tapping into the unlimited offerings of the abundant Universe.

Present Moment Awareness

Among the enlightened beings that have walked this planet, a common message is that the present moment is all we have, and that being stuck in the past or projecting into the future means, without a doubt, that we are living in the mind. Living in the moment is the most challenging of practices, because our wandering mind is constantly creating something for us to fixate on. It's a metaphorical battle as portrayed in the Indian epic *The Bhagavad-Gita,* in which a war is fought between the forces of ego (mind) and the army of the divine consciousness (spirit). In other words, the battle is won through consciously practicing being in the moment and not identifying with, or being controlled by, the fluctuating mind states. It's not an easy practice, and it may take a million tries until we are beyond a doubt living in the present moment at all times; but as we practice, consciousness and awareness gradually enter our lives, and we're guided to our purpose and potential.

Thus, living in the moment will benefit us in many ways, guiding us to our own personal destiny as the ego dissolves. The ego cannot reside in the present moment because it is a product of the past and the future, and we realize this truth as we begin to sit silently and become witnesses to our thoughts. Who is thinking these thoughts? If they can be witnessed, then clearly there is a witnessing presence. Many traditions say that this witness is the divine seeing through us, the source of bliss that we desperately long for as we search for pleasure and fulfillment in the external world. By staying in the present moment and not living in our minds, we come into contact with the divine presence and tap into the unending supply of energy, happiness, and love that is our birthright.

If you're not already familiar with these practices, you may be asking yourself, "How do I live in the present moment?" My favorite tools are my breath and conscious movement, as well as meditation, but it has taken me discipline and many years to make strides in these life-changing practices. It is a universal teaching that bringing your focus to the breath and/or sensations in the body will solidify you in the present moment. Gautam Buddha was said to have used a breathing technique on his path to enlightenment that consisted of being consciously aware of the inhale, the space between the inhale and exhale, the exhale, and the space between the exhale and inhale. I have used this method to bring me back to the present moment many times, as I'm waiting in line, walking, or doing other activities; for if you are constantly engaged with the flow of breath, then you will be undoubtedly residing in the "Now."

Conscious movement has also been a vehicle for me to ride into the present moment. This could be any type of bodily motion, such as yoga, dance, Tai Chi, or martial arts. A deep awakening happens in me when I bring awareness to every sensation in my body during yoga or some other form of meditation in movement. And I try to apply this to my every footstep throughout the day, each complete breath, wherever I go and whatever I'm doing: This is another way to practice being in the now. There is a myriad of great teachers, past and present, who give practical information and insight on how to live in the moment. Surely, if you have the intention, you will be guided to a practice that is right for you.

Anyone can apply these and other techniques to exist in the present moment, but of course, we have to be ready and conscious enough to realize that these concepts and truths will benefit us. A change in our awareness must take place on a gradual basis, starting from where we are in our lives. The shift of awareness is said to be gradual for many reasons, and there is no destination, only a constant unfolding of each perfect moment as we are guided down a river by a force higher than us into the ocean of bliss.

The Pursuit of Happiness and Enlightenment

When I look back, I see that my entire life has been a school of spiritual education; and in the pursuit of happiness, just like every human being, I've made bad choices and had to learn by living with the results of my actions. I can now see the karmic cycle of my life choices leading to suffering because I was ruled by ignorance and ego. But first I had to become aware of this dynamic—to have the awareness to witness the ego and to not be driven by it. Simply bringing consciousness to my thoughts, words, and actions has gradually guided me toward being a balanced, whole person. I now know, thanks to this awareness, that I consciously create the reality that I live in, Heaven or Hell, and that my life path affects others' happiness and peace of mind as well.

My lifelong flight of chaos and renewal has been wrought with mistakes and the hardest of lessons born out of ignorance—lack of knowledge and understanding of what will bring me happiness or suffering. I've also experienced great joy and contentment, mainly after I adopted and embraced the principles of numerous spiritual traditions and rolled them into my own personal manifestation of their teachings. I've learned that on the path of righteousness, there are direct results of my choices and actions, great and small. I've also realized that I can avoid suffering and become a better, happier person by applying age-old tools and principles left for mankind by countless saints, sages, spiritual traditions, religions, and cultures.

By recognizing the divine in myself and in each and every person, I now see that the path is to be of service to others in whatever way possible. This could be a multitude of things, from simply listening to and cheering up a friend in distress, to donating your time or unused goods to those in need. Being of service to others can be as simple as cultivating ourselves to be kind, compassionate, loving individuals; and, most importantly, to give to others what we feel is lacking in our own lives. For instance, if you feel like you're lacking love in your life, explore giving love to friends, family, and acquaintances, and see the results. This in itself will have a far-reaching effect; it is the greatest gift we can bestow, as we're all connected in an incomprehensible way.

With the cultivation of awareness comes the witnessing of the mind's actions, thoughts running through our consciousness like wild horses. A madness has accompanied my thoughts, but I now see that this madness is the mind, or ego, and that within me there is a witness that can watch the mind's action without identifying with it. Many spiritual traditions say that this observer is the divine consciousness that animates our mortal body, and also our spirit, which lives eternally outside of time and space. Most of my life I've been ruled by my ego, cut off from the insight and guidance of my soul. But with patience and discipline, a shift of perspective, and more wisdom from life experiences, I'm now starting to become detached from the mind's wanderings and to awaken to the presence within. In an incredible way that's hard to put into words, this makes my life a blessed paradise regardless of external circumstances.

How do we realize the witness inside of us? While there are many techniques, I've found that meditation, the highest pursuit of countless spiritual faiths, has been the best technique on my passage from darkness to light. Taking the time each day to shut off the mind and sit in stillness has been an invaluable stepping stone to greater health, clarity, well-being, and the realization of my potential. Now I see the mind and its tricks as something that I might not be able to stop or control, but I am able to view my mind from a detached, indifferent standpoint and let it go. I also know through experience that being ruled by the ego is a recipe for suffering and misery, and that only by living an ethical life, making proper choices in the present moment, can I escape unhappiness, regret, and discontent.

Surely I'm not a perfected being, but a work in progress, moving though life at my own pace and still making mistakes and errors of judgment. However, now the mistakes are fewer and farther between, and I have countless tools and techniques to break out of the bondage of depression, sadness, anger, and pain that may confront me. Some of the tools I've found to be helpful in overcoming life's challenges include:

1) Unconditional love and compassion for every living being.
2) Forgiveness of my past actions and others' misdeeds against me, which I now see as the greatest of gifts and teachers.
3) Gratitude: There is always something to be grateful for!
4) Acceptance of "what is."

5) Random acts of kindness, where I give what I can and help a stranger in need, seeing this person as another aspect of the divine.
6) Thinking positively and being optimistic in the face of adversity.
7) Having a sense of humor: This makes life a fabulous comedy.
8) Patience: All things come in good time.
9) Following my heart in all circumstances: The heart will never steer you wrong.
10) Being genuinely happy for others' successes and accomplishments.

The cultivation of happiness and enlightenment is by far the supreme contribution to humanity, and if every person realized this concept and life path, then the world would be a better place. This doesn't suggest that we become a celestial being and float away with a perpetual smile on our face; it simply means that we become alert to how the motion of our life contributes to our inner peace, and also the bliss and freedom of all living beings. But we must begin with working on ourselves: by seeking out and surrounding ourselves with a community of like-minded individuals who can be our extended family as we work toward a joyful, awakened life. In this pursuit of happiness, we may fall back into the pit of hopelessness and pain, but through constant effort and discipline, our individual life path and destiny will be revealed, and a tidal wave of strength will lift us to our highest potential.

This is what I wish for myself and for each and every person, and as I have worked toward this goal, my life has changed in an extreme way. Every day, events and opportunities arise that show me that I'm on the right path, and now that I have locked the door to my past and thrown away the key, there is no turning back. I know that I have traveled too far down this road to walk back, and I feel content to leave it all behind in the mist of time. At the end of my life, I want to have a smile on my face, warmth in my heart, and a twinkle in my eyes, knowing that I made a difference in the world—that in my development of an enlightened path, I made an impact on others, and that I added to the torrent of spiritual growth and love sweeping the planet.

Thank You!

I'd like to send love and gratitude to my family and friends, and those who have supported and assisted me in writing this book: Aymee Coget for her blanket of love and heartfelt guidance, Todd Schafer for his fast and high-quality graphic design services, Kristin Kearns for her masterful editing skills and attention to the tiniest details, and those who took the time to read the advance copies and give me constructive criticism and reviews. More love and a special thank you to Don and Amba Stapleton of the Nosara Yoga Institute, Forest Folger and family, the many teachers under whom I've had the privilege of studying, and all those who have walked before me and offered their wisdom for the benefit of humanity.

I'd also like to give individual thanks and appreciation to all of the body-workers who have helped put my broken body back together, thereby allowing me to be mobile and live a relatively pain-free life: Per Haaland, Adv. Rolfer; Daniel Colfer, DC; Dr. Bobbi Spur; Elsa Etcheverry; and the staff at The Five Branches Institute of TCM.

Biography

Chris is a fifth-generation Californian and currently resides in Northern CA. He is a certified "Interdisciplinary" yoga teacher (E-RYT), a holistic health counselor, and an insatiable world traveler. He spends much of his time surfing, writing, and creating art, while studying a myriad of spiritual traditions. Please feel free to contact Chris at christopherboydlane@hotmail.com

www.ingramcontent.com/pod-product-compliance
Lightning Source LLC
Chambersburg PA
CBHW022006100426
42738CB00041B/355